PASTA HARVEST

PASTA HARVEST

DELICIOUS RECIPES USING VEGETABLES

AT THEIR SEASONAL BEST

BY JANET FLETCHER

PHOTOGRAPHY BY JOHN VAUGHAN

CHRONICLE BOOKS

SAN FRANCISCO

Library of Congress Cataloging-in-Publication Data:
Fletcher, Janet Kessel.
    Pasta harvest: delicious recipes using vegetables
at their seasonal best / by Janet Fletcher;
photography by John Vaughan.
        p. cm.
    Includes index.
    ISBN 0-8118-0567-0
    1. Pasta.   2. Vegetarian cookery.   I. Title.
TX809.M17F55   1995
641.8'22—dc20
94-35148   CIP

Printed in Hong Kong.

Designed by Melanie Doherty Design.

Distributed in Canada by Raincoast Books,
8680 Cambie Street, Vancouver, B.C. V6P 6M9

10 9 8 7 6 5 4 3

Chronicle Books
275 Fifth Street
San Francisco, CA 94103

TABLE OF CONTENTS

FOR DOUG

MY TIRELESS TASTER

ACKNOWLEDGMENTS Several people have shared their time, ideas and expertise with me while I worked on this book. For help with recipes, I would like to thank Barbara Karoff, Mimi Luebbermann, Enzo Polacco and Maria Villa. For help with information on dried pasta, I thank Roland Cook. I am grateful to Elisabetta and Rosa Baldini for their guidance on orecchiette. And I would particularly like to thank all the folks at the Pasta Shop—Erin Andrews, Linda Sikorski, Diana Solari, Juliana Uruburu, Sara Wilson and others— for helping me in many ways on many occasions.

I am also indebted to the people who helped to make this a beautiful book: John Vaughan for his warm and natural photography; to stylists Jody Thompson-Kennedy and Karen Frerichs for making my food look so good on film; and to Melanie Doherty Design for the elegant and imaginative book design. I would also like to acknowledge the artists and merchants who lent items for photography: Biordi Italian Imports, Hastings & Hastings, Nicole Hummer, Sue Fisher King, Aletha Soulé, Summerhouse and Williams-Sonoma.

For her sensitive and thoughtful editing advice on the manuscript, I thank Sharon Silva. And finally, to my editor Bill LeBlond, who helped pull this book idea out of me and has accommodated me at every step, I am deeply grateful.

INTRODUCTION

I HAVE THE GOOD FORTUNE TO LIVE NEAR A THRIVING URBAN MARKETPLACE, A LARGE BUILDING WITH SEVERAL FOOD MERCHANTS UNDER ONE ROOF. THIS WONDERFUL COMPLEX HOUSES A PRODUCE VENDOR, A BUTCHER, A FISHMONGER, A WINE MERCHANT, A BAKERY AND A QUALITY-CONSCIOUS SPECIALTY SHOP THAT SELLS CHEESES, FRESH AND DRIED PASTA, PROSCIUTTO, AND ALL MANNER OF PREPARED AND IMPORTED FOODS.

Not long after I moved into the neighborhood, I realized that I had settled into a near-daily pattern. I would stop at the produce market at the end of the day and buy whatever looked best: fresh asparagus or firm baby artichokes, or a few shiny Japanese eggplants and some ripe local tomatoes. Then I would head for the specialty shop to inspect the rows of packaged pasta, looking for just the right shape to accompany my vegetables. If need be, I would pick up some prosciutto or a tin of anchovies to enhance my sauce.

Back home, I would lay out my purchases and get out the olive oil, garlic and Parmesan. My husband and I would open a bottle of wine and set to work together, trimming artichokes, shelling peas, peeling tomatoes, chopping onions. Usually well within an hour, we were dishing up dinner — steaming plates of pasta with a savory vegetable sauce.

When I realized that we were eating pasta with vegetables several times a week with great pleasure, I began to suspect that there might be an audience for a book on the subject. So many people are looking for ways to assemble healthful meals quickly. And many have now heard about the benefits of the Mediterranean diet, a way of eating based largely on grains (such as pasta), vegetables, dairy products and olive oil. From my own experience, I knew that meals centered around pasta with vegetables could accommodate busy cooks and health concerns in a most enjoyable way.

Spreading that message is this book's chief goal but not its only one. *Pasta Harvest* should also help people who want to explore the less familiar produce in today's supermarkets and farmers' markets. If you've never cooked fennel before, or fava beans, or Swiss chard, you will find that pairing them with pasta provides a delicious and easy introduction. You may also find that familiar vegetables such as broccoli and cauliflower have new appeal when paired with unusual pasta shapes and seasonings. If you currently use a limited range of vegetables at home, this book should expand your horizons.

Lastly, *Pasta Harvest* speaks to those people who think they don't enjoy cooking. I believe that reluctant cooks might change their tune when they see how satisfying and easy it is to assemble a well-balanced pasta dinner—fusilli with broccoli sauce, for example, with some sliced tomatoes first; or perciatelli with a spicy tomato sauce, followed by a green salad. With these simple recipes, preparing dinner can be a pleasure, not a chore. There is something relaxing about peeling fava beans, chopping garlic or slicing mushrooms at the end of a long day. That's when my husband and I share the day's events, reconnecting with each other as we slice and stir and take note of the good aromas building in the kitchen.

Shared with children, these daily rituals might be a little more chaotic but they are no less valuable. My young niece loves to smash and peel garlic, and I get to know her a little better whenever she joins me in the kitchen to make pasta sauce. Youngsters can peel carrots, onions and garlic; pit olives; wash spinach; grate

cheese. Older children can learn to feed fresh pasta dough through a hand-cranked machine. Children who think they don't like spinach or broccoli are much more likely to enjoy it when they've had a hand in its preparation.

Even if you cook alone, you will find these vegetable-sauced pastas a delight to prepare. In fact, for the solo diner, a plate of pasta with vegetables and a glass of wine strikes me as one of the easiest and most healthful meals one can make. Most of the sauces in this book scale down easily, allowing you to make just enough sauce for a single four-ounce serving of pasta. Or you can make enough sauce for eight ounces of pasta but save half of it for the next day. (Please don't precook the pasta!)

Shopping for these pasta meals can be as pleasurable as preparing them. Learn to let the season guide you and to welcome serendipity—to be willing to abandon plans for a broccoli sauce if the peas look better. If you shop at a supermarket, start in the produce department and buy whatever

looks best. Or let the harvest from your garden or a trip to the farmers' market determine dinner. If you keep your pantry well-stocked with pasta shapes, canned tomatoes, chicken stock, anchovies and olive oil, and keep a ready supply of garlic, onions and Parmesan cheese, you can gather the makings for dinner with one stop for produce.

Part of the pleasure I get from these pasta-with-vegetable dishes is watching the seasons march across my plate. In March, I feast on spaghetti tossed with a heap of shredded and browned artichokes (page 45). In June, I toss fresh peas with linguine, prosciutto and mint (page 109). In July, I braise young green beans with tomato to make a sauce for linguine (page 53). In September, between the tomatoes, peppers and eggplant, I could happily eat pasta every day— spaghetti with mixed sweet peppers (page 113); rigatoni with fried eggplant and tomato (page 77); or spaghetti with a refreshing "salad" of tomatoes and goat cheese (page 136). In the fall, I cook rosmarino risotto-style with butternut squash and leeks (page 129) or simmer mushrooms and chestnuts in cream to sauce linguine (page 99). Even winter brings plenty to work with: penne with cauliflower sauce (page 68); linguine with onion sauce (page 86); or homemade buckwheat noodles tossed with braised cabbage, Fontina and sage (page 64).

A simple dinner of pasta with vegetables satisfies so many contemporary needs. The ingredients are wholesome, widely available and relatively inexpensive. Preparation is rarely time-consuming and requires few cooking skills. Those who are trying to cut back on meat will find that a dinner of pasta with vegetables provides plenty of pleasure with no sense of sacrifice. And at a time when fewer families are eating dinner together, these recipes give people reason to gather.

EQUIPPING YOUR KITCHEN A COOK WITH THE MOST RUDIMENTARY KITCHEN CAN PRODUCE DELICIOUS PASTA. ITALIAN GRANDMOTHERS HAVE BEEN DOING IT FOR CENTURIES WITHOUT FOOD PROCESSORS, FANCY POTS OR PROFESSIONAL STOVES. NEVERTHELESS, A FEW INEXPENSIVE TOOLS WILL MAKE PREPARATION EASIER. THE FOLLOWING ITEMS ARE THE ONES I USE OCCASIONALLY OR OFTEN IN PASTA COOKERY.

CHEESE GRATER You can buy electric cheese graters and fancy table-mounted graters and multi-part, hand-cranked graters, but you don't need them. An inexpensive, stand-up four-sided grater works fine. The large holes are good for grating Fontina for Buckwheat Pappardelle with Cabbage, Fontina and Sage (page 64). The medium holes on the grater's narrow side are good for Parmesan, pecorino romano or other hard grating cheeses. Just put a piece of wax paper under the grater and grate away.

COLANDER You need a stainless steel, footed colander that you can stand in the sink when you're ready to drain the pasta pot. If you usually cook with another person, a one-handled stainless steel, wire-mesh sieve can do the job, too; one person holds the sieve while the other—carefully—empties the pasta pot into it.

DOUGH SCRAPER A stainless steel scraper with a rectangular blade and a wooden handle will help you maneuver fresh pasta dough on a work surface and then scrape the surface clean when you're finished.

FOOD MILL A hand-cranked food mill quickly and easily turns canned tomatoes into a smooth, seedless purée. Tomatoes passed through a food mill are the foundation of numerous pasta sauces in this book.

FOOD PROCESSOR A food processor makes quick work of some puréed sauces, such as Fusilli with Broccoli Sauce (page 58), Spaghetti with Sicilian Tomato and Almond Sauce (page 132) and Fusilli with Roasted Red Pepper Cream (page 111). You can also purée canned tomatoes in a food processor, then pass them through a sieve to remove the seeds.

Equipment

MORTAR AND PESTLE With a porcelain or marble mortar and pestle, you can grind spices, garlic or anchovies to a smooth paste. I use it to bruise fennel seed for Perciatelli with Tomato-Fennel Sauce (page 133); to crush peppercorns coarsely for Linguine with Asparagus and Egg (page 46); and to pound peppercorns, garlic, anchovies and butter into a "sauce" for Spaghetti with Grilled Radicchio and Anchovy Butter (page 89).

HAND-CRANKED PASTA MACHINE With a stainless steel hand-cranked pasta machine (mine is Atlas brand), you can turn flour and eggs into beautiful ribbons of fresh pasta in no time. Unlike so many kitchen gadgets, this one is a worthy labor-saving device, one that achieves results as good or better than most people can achieve by hand. The typical machine consists of four parts:

1. A chrome-steel base that rests on the counter and encases two parallel rollers that knead the dough and then gradually flatten it as you bring the rollers closer together (a knob with several settings adjusts the space between the rollers);
2. A C-clamp for fixing the base to a kitchen counter or cutting board;
3. A hand crank that turns the rollers, feeding the pasta through;
4. A pasta-cutting attachment with two sets of grooved rollers, one for cutting ¼-inch-wide noodles (fettuccine), the other for cutting ¹⁄₁₆-inch-wide noodles (tagliolini).

This trusty machine can take years of frequent use if properly cared for. To clean it, use a paintbrush reserved for this task or a dry towel to dust off any particles of flour or dough. Never put it in water or the interior will rust. Keep it covered when not in use.

PASTA POT To provide the pasta plenty of room to move around as it boils, you need a large stainless steel pot with a lid. An 8-quart pot will hold 5 quarts of boiling water comfortably, enough to cook a pound of pasta.

PASTA WHEEL This wooden-handled device, also known as a pastry wheel, has a cutting wheel with a fluted edge. It gives the traditional wavy edges to pappardelle. This is the same tool used to flute the edges of pastry ribbons for a lattice-topped pie.

PEPPER MILL Whole peppercorns ground fresh in a pepper mill have a lively, pungent, invigorating aroma, unlike the lifeless ground pepper sold at the supermarket. Invest in a hand-held pepper mill, buy your peppercorns whole and grind the pepper as you need it.

ROLLING PIN Although I use my Atlas machine to knead and stretch the dough, I use a rolling pin first to flatten the dough enough to feed it through the rollers of the machine. Any wooden or marble pin that you find comfortable will work fine.

SCALE You will find a scale helpful as you make these recipes. To be as accurate as possible, I have given weights, rather than measures, for many ingredients. Because a bunch of broccoli from one market may not weigh the same as a bunch from another, I have generally specified weight after trimming. Weight is also the most accurate measurement for such items as pancetta and prosciutto. After you have made a recipe once or twice, you will probably be comfortable with estimating measures by eye, but for best results the first time, weigh for accuracy. A wall-mounted scale takes up no counter space and will be even more helpful in any baking you do.

SIEVE A large stainless steel, wire-mesh sieve with a handle comes in handy when you want to re-move vegetables such as broccoli from boiling water without draining the water. You can transfer the vegetables with tongs to the sieve and shock them under cold running water, leaving you with a pot of boiling water ready for pasta. See Spaghettini with Escarole, Olives and Anchovies (page 91) for an example of this technique.

SKIMMER A wire-mesh or stainless steel skimmer with a shallow bowl and a long handle is ideal for retrieving vegetables in small pieces, such as broccoli stems and florets, from a large pot of boiling water. After you've removed the vegetables, you can cook the pasta in the same water.

TONGS When you are ready to pull a strand of spaghetti from the boiling water to test for doneness, you need a pair of 12-inch stainless steel tongs. Tongs are also useful for transferring cooked spaghetti, linguine, perciatelli or other long dried pasta shapes from the pot to the serving bowl without draining. As you will notice in the recipes, I use this technique often. It leaves a little water clinging to the pasta, which helps the sauce coat the noodles better.

You can also retrieve long pasta from the pot with a spaghetti rake — a wooden implement that resembles a long-handled hairbrush with a dozen or so wooden "bristles."

GOOD INGREDIENTS FOR GREAT RESULTS CHOOSING INGREDIENTS CAREFULLY IS THE FIRST STEP TO ACHIEVING GOOD RESULTS WITH THESE RECIPES. QUALITY CAN VARY CONSIDERABLY FROM ONE BRAND TO ANOTHER. I ENCOURAGE YOU TO FIND THE BEST SOURCES IN YOUR AREA FOR THE FOLLOWING ITEMS, WHICH YOU WILL USE OFTEN.

ANCHOVIES Most markets sell anchovy fillets packed in olive oil in 2-ounce tins. That is a fine way to buy them. Taste the different brands available in your area to find the one you like best.

Some people say that you can cover any leftover anchovies with olive oil and refrigerate or freeze them. I have never found this to be successful. Within a day — at least to my nose and palate — the anchovies start to oxidize and develop a strong, fishy odor and taste. Since it would be a false economy to use them, I open a fresh tin of anchovies for each dish.

A few specialty stores sell whole salt-packed anchovies in tins. They must be rinsed and filleted before using, but they are delicious — meatier, mellower and (interestingly) less salty tasting than the ones packed in olive oil. The problem is that the tins are large, and unless you cook for crowds, the anchovies will start to taste strong and rancid before you've used many of them. My local Italian market keeps open tins of these salt-packed anchovies and sells them by weight; you buy only as many as you want. If you find anchovies sold this way, and you trust that the market goes through the tin quickly, try them. Just rinse them under cold running water, use your fingers to pry them open along the back and lift out the bones.

CAPERS The unopened flower buds of the Mediterranean caper bush, pickled in brine, add a pleasing salty, vinegary taste to pasta sauce. You can buy them packed in brine or, occasionally, in salt. Salt-packed capers should be rinsed before using. Brine-packed capers can be rinsed or not, as you prefer. In some sauces, I like the briny taste and don't bother to rinse them. Capers come in several sizes, from the tiny nonpareil variety to some almost as large as a pea. There is not a great difference in flavor.

CHEESE Flavorful cheese is an essential ingredient in many pasta-with-vegetable dishes. It provides the satisfying sensation of richness that meat provides in other pasta sauces. A good cheese merchant will have or can get all of the cheeses called for in this book. Many supermarket deli cases will have none of them. If you haven't done so already, seek out a conscientious cheese retailer in your community; he or she will be your ally in achieving the best results with these recipes.

FETA You won't find this moist, crumbly cheese in traditional Italian pasta recipes, but I think its pungent flavor complements sauces with tomatoes, artichokes or sweet peppers. The best feta comes from Greece and Bulgaria, where it is made with sheep's milk (or, occasionally, goat's milk) and is packed in brine. (Ask to have some of the brine; it will keep the cheese fresh longer.) French sheep's milk feta, milder and creamier than feta from Greece or Bulgaria, is a good second choice. Feta from other countries, including American feta, is usually made with cow's milk and lacks the characteristic tang.

FONTINA Although it has many imitators, genuine Fontina comes only from the Val d'Aosta (sometimes written Valle d'Aosta) in northwestern Italy. It is a cow's milk cheese with a creamy texture and a seductive aroma that reminds me of white truffles. Fontina melts beautifully, adding a luxurious richness to pasta dishes.

MOZZARELLA For the recipes in this book, choose a whole-milk mozzarella, domestic or imported, that is firm enough to grate or slice. Polly-O, a nationally distributed brand, is a good choice. It is now possible, in some American cities, to buy fresh, moist whole-milk mozzarella made domestically but in the Italian style. This smooth, milky cheese is delicious with sliced tomatoes, but it is too moist for these recipes. At all costs, avoid the tasteless, rubbery, skim-milk mozzarella that most domestic manufacturers produce.

PARMIGIANO REGGIANO (Parmesan) This is the most useful of pasta cheeses, one you should never be without. It is an aged cow's milk cheese from a tightly defined region of northern Italy, made by strictly controlled measures. You can know you have an authentic Parmigiano Reggiano by the stenciling on the rind ("Parmigiano Reggiano" is stamped around the wheel's perimeter) and by its unique flavor and aroma: it is nutty and brown-buttery with a hint of orange peel.

Most cheese merchants sell several hard grating cheeses that resemble Parmigiano Reggiano, such as American Parmesan, Argentinian Parmesan and Italian grana or Grana Padano. (*Grana* is a generic term for the cow's milk grating cheeses made in the Po Valley of northern Italy. Grana Padano is a more specific name with a legal definition, reserved for grating cheeses from strictly delineated parts of the Po Valley.) These cheeses are always less expensive than Parmigiano Reggiano, and when you taste them, you will know why. They are sharper, more acidic, and without the appealing roundness and mellowness of the more distinguished Parmigiano Reggiano. You can use them in these recipes, but the results will be less pleasing.

Parmesan keeps for several weeks if properly stored. To prevent it from drying out, wrap it tightly before refrigerating. My cheese merchant recommends wrapping it first in waxed paper or butcher paper, then overwrapping with aluminum foil, or wrapping in aluminum foil alone. Plastic wrap can impart its flavor to the outer layer of the cheese after a few days. Always grate Parmesan freshly for each use. Even day-old grated Parmesan has lost a lot of its punch.

PECORINO ROMANO This aged Italian sheep's milk cheese is firm enough to grate. It has a sharp, salty flavor and a pungent taste characteristic of sheep's milk cheese. It is just the right accent for many vegetable-based pasta dishes, particularly those made with green beans, cauliflower, broccoli, fava beans, artichokes, eggplant, arugula or peppers. To store pecorino romano, follow the instructions for Parmesan.

PECORINO TOSCANO (Toscanello) This sheep's milk cheese can be aged until hard, but you are more likely to find it young, when it has the smooth texture of an Emmenthal. It has that unmistakable sheep's milk tang but is milder than pecorino romano. Like pecorino romano, it flatters many vegetables, but I particularly like it with cauliflower (page 67).

FRESH RICOTTA Many American cooks know ricotta as the soft, mild, spoonable cheese that goes in lasagne. But it's useful in several other vegetable sauces for pasta, such as Fusilli with Spinach and Ricotta Sauce (page 123), and in stuffings for pasta shells or cannelloni. (And it doesn't *always* go in lasagne — see page 38.)

The best fresh ricotta is moist, creamy and sweetly fresh. Most of it is made from cow's milk, although you may occasionally find sheep's milk ricotta. Polly-O whole-milk ricotta is a fine product, available in many supermarkets. You may also find that your cheese merchant carries ricotta from a local source, perhaps sold in bulk. If so, ask to taste it first. It is highly perishable and should be avoided if it has started to develop a sour taste.

RICOTTA SALATA This firm, sliceable, creamy-white cheese is made from sheep's milk. It has a grainy texture and a subtle tang. I particularly like its distinctive sheep's milk flavor with eggplant, green beans and zesty tomato sauces.

OLIVE OIL I keep three kinds of olive oil in my kitchen. One is an inexpensive, light-bodied olive oil with a mild flavor. I use it for high-heat cooking, which would compromise the flavor of a better oil, or for delicate sauces that shouldn't have a strong olive oil taste. The second is a moderately priced extra virgin olive oil with more body and a fruitier flavor. This is the oil I use most often for pasta sauces. The third oil is a fine and rather expensive extra virgin olive oil reserved for drizzling atop pasta just before serving. The heat from the noodles releases aromas in the oil, which gives the dish a fragrant lift. You'll note that some recipes call for passing additional oil at the table for that reason; for those situations, use your best extra virgin olive oil. Uncooked sauces, such as Spaghetti with Marinated Tomatoes and Goat Cheese (page 136), also benefit from the best olive oil you can afford.

You may want to be more frugal with your oil than I am and cook primarily with a pure (not extra virgin) olive oil. Where I believe it makes a significant difference, I have specified extra virgin olive oil. Store all your oils away from direct light and heat. Both light and heat accelerate oxidation and rancidity.

OLIVES Both green and ripe (black) olives can enhance pasta sauces with their salty or briny flavors. The following are the varieties I use most often. Try to find a merchant who sells olives in bulk so you can taste before you buy. Olives can vary tremendously from batch to batch.

DRY-CURED These wrinkly black olives, also known as salt-cured or oil-cured olives, are preserved with dry salt rather than brine, then rubbed with olive oil. They have an intense flavor, without the tang that a brine contributes. You can find good dry-cured olives from Morocco, France, Greece, California and elsewhere.

KALAMATA These brine-cured Greek olives should be firm and relatively mild. If they are mushy, excessively salty or vinegary, choose another brand or another olive.

NIÇOISE Despite their name, these small brine-cured ripe olives may come from countries other than France. Whatever their source, they should be firm and mild, with only a subtle brine flavor.

PICHOLINE These sleek brine-cured green olives have an appealing crispness and a nutty flavor. They may be from France, or they may be grown in other countries and cured in this French style.

PANCETTA Pancetta is unsmoked Italian slab bacon seasoned with salt, pepper and other spices, and then cured. For curing, it is usually rolled up like a rug and tied to fix it in a thick sausage shape. When you buy it, it will be sliced crosswise into rounds that uncoil.

I usually ask to have it sliced about ¼ inch thick so that it will dice easily. It will keep for a few days in the refrigerator if well wrapped.

You'll find pancetta in Italian markets and in the delicatessen of well-stocked supermarkets. Because of its smoky taste, American bacon is not a good substitute but it will work in a pinch.

HOT RED PEPPER FLAKES These piquant pepper flakes are ground dried red chilies (*peperoncini*). They give a welcome kick to many vegetable sauces for pasta. You can grind them yourself in a spice grinder from whole dried red chilies, or you can buy them already ground. Brands and batches vary in pungency, which makes it hard to specify a quantity in a recipe. I typically use ¼ teaspoon in a sauce for a pound of pasta, but you may find that your brand or your taste suggests another level.

DRIED PORCINI The wild mushrooms known in Italy as *porcini (Boletus edulis)* can be successfully dried. You will find them sold in bulk or packaged at specialty-food stores that carry Italian products. Dried porcini have an intense, woodsy flavor that enriches tomato- and cream-based sauces. They may seem expensive, but a little goes a long way. Store them in a tightly covered container at room temperature and they will keep indefinitely.

Dried porcini must be reconstituted in warm water before use. Soak them until they soften, about 1 hour. Use enough water so that any grit the mushrooms harbor can sink to the bottom. When softened, lift them out of the water with a slotted spoon to leave any grit behind. Strain the soaking liquid through dampened cheesecloth and add to sauces as recipe specifies.

PROSCIUTTO It was a red letter day when the U. S. government finally allowed the importation of true prosciutto di Parma—the salt-cured, air-dried ham from Italy. Until the late 1980s, we had to be satisfied with the inferior domestic commercial product. I suspect that it won't be long before we have American prosciutti as good as the Italian: at least one California entrepreneur is making fine ones on a small scale now. In the meantime, I recommend using imported prosciutto di Parma. It is expensive, but most of these recipes call for only a few ounces. I buy it sliced a little thicker than is traditional for antipasto, so that it's easier to julienne or mince. Prosciutto dries out quickly after slicing; try to buy it the day you need it.

STOCK Several of the recipes in this book depend on chicken stock to add flavor and moisture to a sauce. Fortunately, there are some good canned stocks available (and some ghastly ones, too). Compare brands critically. I like Swanson Clear Chicken Broth with ⅓ Less Salt. If I want only a subtle meat flavor, however, even this relatively delicate broth is too intense. For those recipes, I dilute the stock with water.

Vegetarians can substitute vegetable broth or even water for chicken stock. When a nationally distributed manufacturer comes up with a tasty canned vegetable broth, it will be a major advance. I have yet to find one that appeals to me.

CANNED TOMATOES Top-quality canned tomatoes can produce delicious pasta sauces. For much of the year, they are a better choice than fresh tomatoes. Commercial canners harvest and process tomatoes at the height of their summer ripeness; no wonder they have better flavor than the fresh-market winter tomatoes grown in Mexico or Florida and picked underripe so they can be shipped long distances.

Experiment with the canned tomato brands available to you to find the one you like best. It may not be fair to judge a brand on the basis of one can, but if you try a few cans of each brand, you will probably find some that have consistently superior flavor and texture. I prefer a California brand (distributed nationwide) called Muir Glen; the tomatoes taste riper, richer and less acidic than most other brands I have tried — even better than the famed San Marzano–type canned tomatoes from Italy.

It's not worth skimping on canned tomatoes, which are rarely expensive anyway. Thin-tasting, acidic canned tomatoes make thin-tasting, acidic sauces that you can never correct.

For most pasta sauces, I use strained canned tomatoes. To make them, I pass the tomatoes through a food mill into a stainless steel bowl. This eliminates the seeds and any bits of skin or tough core and yields a smooth tomato purée. If you don't have a food mill, you can purée the tomatoes in a food processor, then pass them through a sieve. This froths them up a bit and probably crushes some of the bitter seeds, so it is a less desirable but acceptable alternative. You can also just chop them very finely, removing any tough bits around the stem; that won't eliminate the seeds, but for many sauces, that doesn't matter.

FRESH TOMATOES Generally, fresh ripe plum tomatoes make better tomato sauce than large, juicy slicing tomatoes. That's because plum tomatoes, sometimes called Roma tomatoes, are bred expressly for sauce. They have thick, meaty pulp and not much juice, so they cook down quickly. For that reason, I specify plum tomatoes for many of the recipes in this book that call for cooking fresh tomatoes. You can use slicing tomatoes, but they may take longer to cook down, and the sauce will probably not be as thick and rich. For uncooked pasta sauces, such as Spaghetti with Marinated Tomatoes and Goat Cheese (page 136), I prefer to use slicing tomatoes because of their full, ripe flavor. If the recipe doesn't specify the type of tomatoes, use whatever kind look and smell best in your market.

Do you need to peel tomatoes? Not always. I don't mind a bit of peel in some of the more rustic pasta sauces. After the sauce has simmered for 15 minutes or so, the peel is soft and unobjectionable. You'll find several sauces in this book that use unpeeled tomatoes. Of course, you can peel the tomatoes if you prefer.

TO PEEL AND SEED TOMATOES Bring a large pot of water to a boil. Fill a bowl three-fourths full with ice water. Cut a skin-deep X in the rounded end of each tomato. Place tomatoes in boiling water for about 30 seconds. Very ripe tomatoes will need even less time; not-quite-ripe tomatoes a few seconds longer. If you have a lot of tomatoes to peel, do them in batches so the water remains at a boil. Using a slotted spoon, transfer blanched tomatoes to ice water. When cool, slip off the skin from each tomato; it should peel back easily from the X. Core tomatoes. Halve plum tomatoes through the stem; halve slicing tomatoes horizontally. Use your fingers to pull the seeds and juice out of the seed cavities.

MAKING FRESH PASTA

ALTHOUGH FRESH EGG PASTA IS WIDELY AVAILABLE NOW FROM SPECIALTY STORES, IT IS EXTREMELY SATISFYING TO MAKE YOUR OWN. ONCE YOU HAVE MASTERED THE METHOD— WHICH IS NOT AT ALL DIFFICULT—YOU WILL PROBABLY FIND THAT YOUR OWN NOODLES TASTE BETTER AND FRESHER THAN THOSE YOU CAN BUY. MANY (ALTHOUGH NOT ALL) FRESH PASTA MANUFACTURERS USE PRECRACKED, PASTEURIZED EGGS INSTEAD OF FRESH EGGS. ALSO, GIVEN THE REALITIES OF MANUFACTURING AND DISTRIBUTION, THE PASTA YOU BUY AT A RETAIL SHOP MAY HAVE BEEN MADE MANY HOURS—SOMETIMES DAYS—BEFORE.

Nevertheless, store-bought fresh pasta is a welcome convenience, and I use it often. If you have the luxury of choice, look for a local manufacturer who uses fresh eggs and who sells the pasta within 24 hours of making it.

Here is the method for making fresh pasta in your own kitchen. You need little more than a work surface, a pasta machine (see page 13) and a rolling pin. It is difficult to say exactly how much flour you will need; it depends in part on the moisture content of the flour and in part on the size of your eggs. I find that 3 extra-large eggs absorb 2¼ to 2½ cups flour, but you may find that you need a little less or a little more.

To make about 1 pound fresh noodles:
Approximately 2½ cups flour
3 extra-large eggs, blended with a fork
Semolina, for dusting baking sheets and noodles

Put 2½ cups flour in a mound on your work surface. With your hand, make a well in the center large enough to contain the beaten eggs. Make sure the flour "walls" around the well are sturdy enough to keep the eggs from running out. Pour the eggs into the well. Using a fork held with the tines parallel to the work surface, begin stirring the eggs and drawing in flour from the sides, using your other hand to shore up the walls. Work carefully to avoid making a hole in the flour walls that would allow the egg to run out.

When you have incorporated enough flour so that you can no longer work easily with a fork, you can begin to incorporate flour gently with your hands, kneading the mixture lightly. When the dough has the texture of a firm biscuit dough, use a metal scraper to pick it up off the work surface and set it aside. Scrape up all the flour on your work surface — you will probably still have about ½ cup — and sieve it to remove any crumbly bits that the dough will no longer absorb readily. Discard them. For the same reason, wash your hands to remove any caked-on bits and dry your hands well.

Return the dough to the work surface with the sieved flour alongside. Knead gently with your hands, adding flour as necessary, until the dough feels firm and dry enough to go through the pasta machine. Shape it into a rectangle narrow enough to go through your machine, using a rolling pin to flatten it. Cut the dough in half widthwise. (You can leave it whole, but I find it easier to work with small pieces.) Cover one-half with a dish towel.

To knead and stretch the other half, firmly clamp your pasta machine to an immovable surface. Set the rollers on the widest setting. Flour the dough liberally and use a rolling pin to flatten it enough to go through the rollers. Feed it through one time. Lay the resulting ribbon down and flour it, then fold it in thirds, matching edges up to make a neat rectangle. With the rolling pin, roll it out gently in the other direction (with the open ends at top and bottom), flouring as necessary to keep it from sticking. By flattening the dough gently on one side and then on the other, you can keep the open ends matched up so you continue to have a neat rectangle. With the roller still on the widest setting, repeat the process nine times: feeding the dough through, flouring and folding the ribbon in thirds, then flouring lightly and flattening. With each successive trip through the rollers, you should need less flour. At the end of this mechanical kneading process, you should have a smooth, silky, well-blended ribbon of dough. Cover it with a towel and let it rest for 15 minutes.

Now you are ready to begin the stretching process by feeding the ribbon through progressively narrower settings, beginning again with the widest one. Cut the ribbon into manageable lengths whenever it gets too unwieldy, and flour it lightly as needed to keep it from sticking to the rollers. I find that setting number 5 — the next-to-last setting — on the Atlas machine is thin enough. Setting number 6 is too thin. As each sheet passes through the final setting, lay it on a lightly floured dish towel or on a fine-mesh rack. The sheets need to dry for about 15 minutes before cutting to prevent the cut noodles from sticking together.

While you wait for the first batch of sheets to dry, repeat the kneading and stretching process with the second half of the dough. When all the dough sheets feel dry enough to feed through the cutting attachment (but not *too* dry, or they will crack in the cutter), cut them into fettuccine (¼ inch wide) or tagliolini (¹⁄₁₆ inch wide). Arrange the noodles on baking sheets sprinkled with semolina, and toss them gently with semolina to keep them from sticking to each other or the baking sheet. Cover with a dish towel and let rest for an hour before cooking.

To cut noodles by hand, when a sheet feels dry enough to cut without sticking, roll it into a loose roll about 3 inches wide, then use a sharp chef's knife to cut noodles of desired width. Because the home pasta machine's cutting attachment has only two widths, you will need to cut the noodles by hand if you want linguine (⅛ inch wide) or pappardelle (½ inch wide).

You can make fresh noodles 3 or 4 hours ahead and keep them at cool room temperature, covered with a towel. You can also freeze fresh pasta, homemade or store-bought, with some success. Freeze it in a sturdy plastic bag and cook directly from the freezer; do not thaw first.

IT IS AMAZING TO ME THAT A PRODUCT THAT CONSISTS ONLY OF FLOUR AND WATER CAN VARY SO MUCH FROM ONE MANUFACTURER TO ANOTHER. IF YOU DOUBT IT, INVITE SOME FRIENDS TO A BLIND TASTING OF COOKED SPAGHETTI SEASONED ONLY WITH A LITTLE OLIVE OIL AND SALT. YOU WILL SEE OBVIOUS DIFFERENCES IN APPEARANCE AND TASTE REMARKABLE VARIATIONS IN TEXTURE FROM BRAND TO BRAND.

Dried egg pasta aside, the best packaged dried pasta contains only semolina and water. Semolina is a coarse, pale yellow flour milled from durum wheat, which is higher in protein than the wheat used for all-purpose flour. It makes a sturdy noodle that has a firm, chewy texture when cooked. In Italy, the best manufacturers buy their semolina carefully, often blending several types to get the texture they want.

The methods used to knead, dry and cut the pasta also influence quality. In general, the best Italian manufacturers knead their dough longer and dry the noodles at lower temperatures than American manufacturers do, resulting in better texture and flavor. With some domestic brands, the boiling noodles taste mushy on the outside before they are done inside.

The best manufacturers cut their pasta by forcing it through bronze dies, which give the noodle a rough texture. Teflon-coated dies, which other manufacturers use, give a smooth, somewhat slippery texture. Not surprisingly, the rough-textured noodles hold a sauce better and are more pleasing to the tongue. It is instructive to look at various brands of spaghetti under a magnifying glass to see the textural differences.

I have yet to find a domestic pasta brand that measures up to the Italian imports. What's more, some American manufacturers suggest cooking times that are ridiculously long. I encourage you to buy only imported Italian pasta, such as the widely available De Cecco brand. De Cecco pasta, cut with bronze dies, comes in a wide variety of shapes and is not expensive.

WHICH SHAPE FOR WHICH SAUCE?

WHEN YOU HAVE COOKED AND EATEN PASTA FOR A LONG TIME, THE PAIRING OF SHAPE TO SAUCE BECOMES ALMOST INSTINCTIVE. THE MATCHES ARE NOT MADE HAPHAZARDLY, BUT WITH A SENSITIVITY TO THE SUBTLE FACTORS THAT MAKE A HAPPY MARRIAGE.

That's why this book is not a collection of sauces, but a collection of dishes — eighty-seven pleasing pairings of sauce and shape. When you see how nicely a smooth broccoli sauce seeps into the "valleys" of spiral-shaped fusilli (page 58), you'll understand why that's a natural match. You could use the same sauce on penne, but it wouldn't cling to the pasta in such a satisfying way. The latter is a good marriage; the former is great.

Until you have developed your own sense of what goes with what, refined through experience, the following outline can guide you. If you want to use a shape other than the one(s) specified in these recipes, check this list for appropriate substitutes. In general, a sauce that works with spaghetti will work nicely with other long dried shapes, such as linguine or perciatelli. A sauce paired in this book with penne rigate will work best with other short, stubby shapes such as gemelli, cavatappi or rigatoni.

Here's another "in general": Dried pasta can support sturdier sauces than fresh pasta. A thick, zesty tomato sauce that would weigh down delicate fettuccine will find the strong partner it needs in perciatelli, penne or rigatoni. Which isn't to say that tomato sauce never goes with fresh pasta. It often does. Everyone has had lasagne layered with tomato sauce and cheese. And a smooth tomato sauce enriched with cream is a wonderful coating for pappardelle (see page 143).

If you wonder whether a sauce will go with a particular shape, imagine it on your plate and on your tongue: Will it be easy to maneuver pasta and sauce together? You will be chasing fresh peas around on your plate all night if you pair them with penne; it's a lot easier to trap peas in the hollows of gnocchi or conchiglie or to enfold them in ribbons of soft fresh linguine.

LONG NOODLES ✿ SPAGHETTINI Because of their thinness, these noodles go best with simple, delicate sauces: arugula, garlic and olive oil; fresh tomato, basil and butter; shredded and sautéed artichokes.

SPAGHETTI The most versatile long noodle; good with cooked and uncooked tomato sauces, pesto, grilled vegetables, wilted greens, sweet peppers.

PERCIATELLI OR BUCATINI This thick, hollow noodle shows best with rustic, highly seasoned tomato sauces.

LINGUINE Flat noodles that wrap nicely around small pieces of soft vegetables, such as asparagus, cauliflower, artichokes, julienned zucchini or sweet peppers. Also good with pesto and similar pastelike sauces.

VERMICELLI, CAPELLINI / CAPELLI D'ANGELO (ANGEL'S HAIR) These fine noodles are too delicate to support most vegetable sauces.

SHORT STUBBY PASTA *CANNARONI, GEMELLI, GNOCCHETTI, PENNE, PENNE RIGATE, PENNONI, RIGATONI, SEDANI, TORTIGLIONI* Suited to chunky, tomato-based vegetable sauces and to baked pasta dishes with béchamel.

SHORT PASTA WITH HOLLOWS *CONCHIGLIE, FARFALLE, GNOCCHI, LUMACHE* Ideal with chunky vegetable sauces with peas, chick-peas, dried beans, lentils or other ingredients that can slip into the hollows.

MISCELLANEOUS SHAPES *ORECCHIETTE* Sauces with chopped broccoli, broccoli rabe, cauliflower, fresh and dried shelling beans.

FUSILLI AND RUOTE (sometimes called rotelle) Thick, creamy vegetable purées that slip into the grooves and hollows.

FRESH PASTA In general, fresh pasta is a good choice for cream sauces, butter-based sauces, brothy sauces or delicate sauces made with tender spring vegetables like peas, fava beans and asparagus. And fresh pasta is essential to lasagne, of course.

Narrow fresh noodles such as linguine need the most delicate sauces. Wider noodles, such as fettuccine or pappardelle, can take a sauce with a little more substance.

If you are cutting pasta by hand, you can make noodles as narrow or wide as you like. If you are buying fresh pasta from a specialty store that makes its own, you will probably have a choice of three or four widths (and the option of buying the whole sheet and cutting it yourself). Unfortunately, there is no standardization of pasta terms in these stores. One store's fettuccine is another's tagliatelle. Many of these stores and many supermarkets sell a narrow fresh noodle labeled "linguine," a concept that doesn't exist in Italy where linguine is always dried. It is usually about ⅛ inch wide, a size I find useful for many pasta sauces.

For clarity, I offer my own definitions below. If you are buying fresh pasta for these recipes, buy noodles of the suggested width regardless of their name. Even Italians often disagree about the "right" width and the "right" names for the various fresh pastas.

❂ **TAGLIOLINI, TAGLIARINI, TAGLIERINI** These names all refer to ¹⁄₁₆-inch-wide noodles. The narrow cutter on the hand-cranked Atlas home pasta machine yields noodles this size. I find them too delicate for most vegetable sauces. They are more appropriate for soup.

❂ **LINGUINE** These noodles are about ⅛ inch wide. They are perfect for delicate sauces containing peas or leeks, or small pieces of vegetable such as chopped fennel or grated zucchini.

❂ **FETTUCCINE** These ¼-inch-wide noodles can accommodate slightly heavier vegetable sauces, such as those made with mushrooms, braised green beans or artichokes. The wider cutter on the hand-cranked Atlas home pasta machine yields noodles this size.

❂ **PAPPARDELLE** These ½-inch-wide noodles can support a moderately robust sauce, such as the combination of braised cabbage, Fontina and sage on page 64. They also take nicely to cream sauces, such as the cream-enriched tomato sauce on page 143.

ILLUSTRATED GUIDE TO PASTA SHAPES

FRESH EGG PASTA

Taliolini / Tagliarini

Linguine

Fettuccine

Pappardelle

DRIED PASTA

Spaghettini

Spaghetti

Linguine

Perciatelli / Bucatini

DRIED PASTA

Rigatoni

Ditali

Gnocchi

Penne Rigate

Conchiglie Rigate

Orecchiette

Pennoni

Rosmarino

Gemelli

Gnocchetti Rigati

Farfalle

Cavatappi

Fusilli

Cannaroni Rigati

COOKING PASTA

TO COOK PROPERLY, PASTA NEEDS TO FLOAT FREELY IN A GENEROUS QUANTITY OF BOILING SALTED WATER. FOR 1 POUND OF PASTA, USE 4 TO 5 QUARTS OF WATER, OR EVEN 6 QUARTS IF YOUR POT IS BIG ENOUGH. PURISTS SAY YOU MUST START WITH COLD WATER, BUT MY PALATE ISN'T THAT REFINED. I OFTEN FILL MY POT WITH HOT WATER TO SAVE TIME.

Bring the water to a rolling boil and add 1 tablespoon of salt. The salt flavors the pasta slightly. (The salt's purpose is not, as some suggest, to raise the boiling point of the water and thus cook the pasta faster. You would have to add much more than 1 tablespoon salt to change the temperature of 5 quarts of water appreciably.)

Add the pasta all at once. If you are cooking long dried strands, such as spaghetti, you may not be able to submerge the full length of the strands immediately, but they will soften in seconds. Use a wooden spoon or tongs to coax them down into the pot. Never break long pasta to fit it into the pot. Twirling long strands around your fork is part of the pleasure of eating spaghetti.

Give the pasta one good stir, then cover until the water comes back to a boil. Uncover and continue to cook at a vigorous boil, stirring every so often to make sure no pasta is sticking to the bottom of the pot. You may need to keep the pot partially covered to maintain a boil.

When is it done? The phrase *al dente* ("to the tooth") says it all: the pasta should be firm—but not hard—under your tooth. To achieve that, it must be drained when it offers just a slight core of resistance. Don't wait until that bit of firmness is gone, or your pasta will be overcooked by the time you have drained it. I find the cooking times indicated on packages of dried Italian pasta (specifically, De Cecco and Delverde brands) to be generally accurate, but I never depend on them. I start to taste for doneness about a minute before the package suggests and may test a piece every 15 or 20 seconds after that. I am looking for that perfect moment when it still resists but just barely.

Fresh pasta cooks quickly—and the fresher, the faster. Homemade fresh pasta, 1 hour old, will cook in seconds. Store-bought fresh pasta may need 30 seconds or so after the pot returns to the boil. Test, test, test. And remember that the pasta will continue to cook while you are hauling the pot over to the sink and draining it. Remove it from the heat before you think it's done. Like dried pasta, properly cooked fresh pasta should still offer some firmness to the tooth.

Before you are ready to drain the pot, put a colander in the sink. Drain the pasta all at once and shake the colander once or twice. Shells (conchiglie) and gnocchi need an extra shake because they trap water. It is a mistake to think that pasta needs to be shaken dry, however. On the contrary, it should be left a little wet to help the sauce coat the noodles nicely.

There is another way to drain pasta, which is not to drain it at all. Long strands like spaghetti, spaghettini or linguine can be lifted out with tongs or a pasta rake and transferred, dripping wet, directly to the serving bowl. This is the method I prefer: it's easy and it leaves me with plenty of hot pasta water if I need to thin the sauce even further. Fresh pasta is usually too fragile to treat this way. It should be drained rapidly in a sieve or colander.

Never rinse cooked pasta. Rinsing would cool it off and remove the surface starch that helps the sauce to adhere.

SAUCING PASTA AFTER THE PASTA IS DRAINED, THE OBJECT IS TO GET IT TO THE TABLE AS QUICKLY AND AS HOT AS POSSIBLE. YOU CAN TURN THE DRAINED PASTA DIRECTLY INTO THE SKILLET THAT HOLDS THE SAUCE AND TOSS THE TWO TOGETHER IN THE SKILLET. OR YOU CAN RETURN THE DRAINED PASTA TO THE PASTA POT OR PLACE IT IN A WARM, SHALLOW BOWL, ADD THE SAUCE, AND TOSS THE TWO TOGETHER. I USUALLY USE THE LATTER METHODS BECAUSE THE PASTA IS EASIER TO TOSS IN A LARGE POT OR BOWL THAN IN A CROWDED SKILLET.

You may find that the recipes in this book call for less sauce than you are accustomed to. This is in keeping with Italian — and my own — taste. Ideally, there is just enough sauce to coat the noodles lightly, with no puddle left at the bottom of the bowl. With tomato- and cream-based sauces, that is what I aim for. Oil-based sauces with chopped vegetables — such as Orecchiette with Broccoli (page 59) — are a little different since these sauces don't "coat" the pasta in the same way. For these sauces, I use just enough oil or fat to give the noodles an even gloss.

When you toss pasta and sauce together, you must make a critical call: Is the sauce moist enough? If not, you can add a tablespoon or two—or even several tablespoons—of hot water reserved from cooking the pasta. Fresh noodles in particular soak up a lot of sauce and continue to do so for several minutes after tossing. Add hot water as necessary to keep them from being gummy or dry. Grated cheese also thickens sauces. A dish of sauced pasta that you thought was just right may look too dry after you add the cheese; if so, add a few tablespoons of water to moisten it. It is not uncommon in Italy for the cook to put a pitcher of hot water on the table for diners to moisten their pasta to taste.

A NOTE ABOUT SEASONING Because cooked pasta is bland, the sauce you add to it should be highly seasoned. The sauce that tastes a little aggressive in the skillet will probably taste just right when spread over cooked noodles. In particular, I find it all too easy to undersalt a pasta sauce. In my experience, a sauce needs to be generously salted for the dish to taste right once the noodles are added. Of course, salt tolerance varies among individuals, which is why I have avoided giving precise salt measurements. And all salt is not alike: I use kosher salt, which tastes milder than conventional iodized table salt. Season your sauce to your taste, but remember that noodles have little or no salt.

SERVING PASTA WHEN PASTA AND SAUCE ARE WELL MINGLED, TRANSFER INDIVIDUAL PORTIONS TO SERVING DISHES WARMED IN THE OVEN. I ALMOST NEVER SERVE PASTA FAMILY STYLE—LETTING GUESTS HELP THEMSELVES FROM A LARGE BOWL. IT IS TOO AWKWARD AT THE TABLE, IT TAKES TOO LONG AND PASTA AND SAUCE DON'T ALWAYS GET SERVED IN THE PROPER PROPORTIONS, LEAVING THE LAST PERSON WITH A LITTLE PASTA AND A LOT OF SAUCE OR VICE VERSA. IF YOU WANT TO SERVE FAMILY STYLE—ON A BUFFET FOR A LARGE GROUP, FOR EXAMPLE—CHOOSE A RECIPE THAT PAIRS A SHORT PASTA SHAPE (RIGATONI, PENNE OR FUSILLI, FOR EXAMPLE) WITH A SMOOTH SAUCE THAT CLINGS TO THE PASTA. FUSILLI WITH BROCCOLI SAUCE (PAGE 58), RIGATONI WITH NEAPOLITAN TOMATO SAUCE (PAGE 151) OR FUSILLI WITH RED PEPPER CREAM SAUCE (PAGE 111) WOULD BE GOOD CHOICES.

Pasta is traditionally served in broad, shallow bowls, to make eating easier. The sloping sides of the bowl give you something to twirl your fork against. Whether you use bowls or dinner plates, be sure to warm them first.

SERVES HOW MANY? IT DEPENDS Most of the recipes in this book use about 1½ pounds of vegetables to make a sauce for 1 pound of pasta. These proportions yield a completed dish that serves four generously as a main course. If the sauce consists primarily of a green vegetable—as for Orecchiette with Broccoli (page 59) or Spaghetti with Shredded Artichokes (page 45)—then the completed dish is, to my mind, a completely satisfying and balanced family dinner. We may nibble on some olives, radishes or breadsticks while we cook, or have a small cheese course afterward (especially if there was little or no cheese in the pasta), but otherwise these green-vegetable–sauced pastas are one-dish family meals at my house.

If the sauce doesn't include a green vegetable, or not very much of one, such as Perciatelli with Spicy Tomato Sauce (page 141), I usually add a green salad before or after to complete the meal. With a salad, these recipes serve six.

Italians typically serve pasta as a first course, followed by a meat or fish course. In that context, these recipes serve six generously—or even eight if the rest of the meal is substantial. But most Americans—myself included—have embraced the idea of pasta as the main event; that is how I serve all the recipes in this book. For casual dinners with friends, pasta is a wonderful main course because everyone relaxes when eating it. It is hard to be reserved or formal with a plate of pasta in front of you.

EATING PASTA WITH MANY PASTA SHAPES, THERE IS NO QUESTION ABOUT HOW TO EAT THEM. YOU SPEAR PENNE OR FUSILLI WITH A FORK. YOU CUT INTO DELICATE LASAGNE WITH THE SIDE OF YOUR FORK. BUT SPAGHETTI, LINGUINE AND OTHER LONG PASTAS PRESENT A CHALLENGE TO DINERS CONCERNED ABOUT MAKING A MESS OR LOOKING UNMANNERLY.

Learning to twirl spaghetti or linguine on a fork, Italian style, adds to the pleasure of eating them. Put away spoon and knife: you don't need either. Just capture a few strands of pasta in the tines of your fork, twirl them into a ball while holding the fork against the bowl and lift the whole ensemble to your mouth. It's okay if a few strands dangle. A little slurping is acceptable; cutting the pasta is not.

a

ARTICHOKES / ASPARAGUS

ARTICHOKES

FOR PASTA SAUCES, I USUALLY USE THE EGG-SHAPED "BABY" ARTICHOKES AVAILABLE IN MARKETS IN SPRING AND FALL. THEY ARE MORE TENDER THAN THE BIG ARTICHOKES AND THERE IS LESS WASTE. THESE LITTLE ARTICHOKES—USUALLY 1½ TO 2 OUNCES—AREN'T IMMATURE VERSIONS OF THE BIG ONES; THEY ARE FULLY MATURE ARTICHOKES THAT GROW LOW ON THE PLANT, WHERE THEY DON'T GET MUCH SUN. IF THEY'RE LESS THAN ABOUT 2 OUNCES, THEY WON'T HAVE DEVELOPED A FUZZY INTERIOR CHOKE; AFTER EXTERNAL TRIMMING, YOU CAN EAT THE WHOLE THING. ✐ YOU CAN USE LARGE ARTICHOKES IN THESE RECIPES, ALTHOUGH YOU WILL NEED TO REMOVE THE CHOKE (SEE BELOW) AND YOU MAY HAVE TO COOK THEM A LITTLE LONGER. WHETHER YOU ARE BUYING LARGE OR SMALL ONES, LOOK FOR ARTICHOKES THAT FEEL FIRM, NOT SQUISHY; THEY SHOULD BE HEAVY FOR THEIR SIZE. I USUALLY BUY A COUPLE EXTRA IN CASE SOME OF THEM HAVE BAD SPOTS INSIDE.

Artichokes of any size may look forbidding if you have never trimmed them before, but trimming is easy. Once you have done it a couple times, you will get fast at it.

To trim baby artichokes (1½ to 2 ounces each), fill a bowl with cold water; add the juice of half a lemon. Peel back the outer leaves on each artichoke until they break off at the base. Keep removing leaves until you reach the pale green heart. Cut about ⅓ inch off the top of the heart to remove the pointed leaf tips; cut away any stem. Trim the base to remove any dark green parts. Immediately drop the trimmed hearts into the acidulated water to prevent browning.

For larger artichokes, fill a bowl with cold water; add the juice of half a lemon. Peel back the tough outer artichoke leaves until they break off at the base. Keep removing leaves until you reach the ones that are at least half pale green, with darker green tips. (Discard the leaves or steam them and eat them with mayonnaise or vinaigrette.) Slice off the top inch or so of the artichoke to remove the dark green tips. Cut off all but ¾ inch of the stem. With a small, sharp knife, cut away the dark green outer layer of the stem and any dark green parts on the base to reveal the pale, tender inner part. Cut trimmed artichoke in half lengthwise. Use a spoon to dig out the hairy choke, including the very fine inner leaves with prickly tips. Transfer artichokes to acidulated water to prevent browning.

ARTICHOKE LASAGNE

NO APOLOGIES FOR THE LENGTH OF THIS RECIPE: IT IS ABSOLUTELY WORTH THE EFFORT. LIKE ALL LASAGNES, IT TAKES TIME TO ASSEMBLE, BUT THEN IT CAN STAND FOR AN HOUR OR TWO BEFORE BAKING. (DON'T REFRIGERATE IT UNLESS YOU PLAN TO HOLD IT LONGER THAN THAT.)

IF YOU USE SHEETS OF STORE-BOUGHT PASTA, YOU WILL PROBABLY NEED TO ROLL THEM THINNER AT HOME. I PASS THEM THROUGH THE NUMBER 5 SETTING ON AN ATLAS PASTA MACHINE. PLEASE DON'T OMIT THIS STEP. IT IS IN PART THE THINNESS OF THE NOODLE LAYERS THAT MAKES THIS LASAGNE SO DELICATE AND APPEALING.

YOU NEED ONLY ABOUT 3/4 POUND PASTA FOR THIS RECIPE, BUT IT'S WISE TO HAVE SOME EXTRA ON HAND IN CASE NOODLES TEAR DURING ROLLING OR COOKING.

For the béchamel:

· *4 tablespoons unsalted butter*

· *5 tablespoons all-purpose flour*

· *2½ cups milk*

· *½ cup chicken stock*

· *2 fresh thyme sprigs*

· *1 bay leaf*

· *½ cup freshly grated Parmesan cheese*

· *Salt and freshly ground black pepper*

❧ To make béchamel, melt butter in a medium saucepan over moderate heat. Add flour and whisk to blend. Cook, whisking constantly, for a minute or two, then add milk, stock, thyme sprigs and bay leaf. Bring to a simmer, whisking often; mixture will thicken considerably. When sauce simmers, reduce heat to lowest setting and cook, stirring occasionally with a wooden spoon, about 15 minutes to draw the flavors out of the seasonings. Remove from heat; remove and discard herbs. Stir in Parmesan and season with salt and pepper.

❧ To make tomato sauce, heat olive oil in a 10-inch skillet over moderately low heat. Add garlic and sauté 1 minute to release its fragrance. Add tomatoes and thyme. Season with salt and pepper and sugar if tomatoes seem too tart.

Bring to a simmer, then adjust heat to maintain a simmer. Cook, stirring occasionally, until mixture is thick and tasty, about 15 minutes.

❧ Drain artichokes, then chop them into neat small dice. Heat olive oil in a 12-inch skillet over moderate heat. Add artichokes, season well with salt and pepper and stir to coat with fat. Add stock and bring to a simmer. Cover, adjust heat to maintain a simmer and cook until artichokes are quite tender and liquid has evaporated, about 15 minutes. Uncover occasionally and stir to make sure artichokes aren't sticking to the skillet. When they are tender, add garlic and cook 1 minute, stirring, to release its fragrance. Transfer artichokes to a medium bowl. Add béchamel and toss to blend. Taste and adjust seasoning.

For the tomato sauce:

· 2 tablespoons olive oil

· 2 large cloves garlic, minced

· 1½ cups strained canned tomatoes (pages 21–22)

· ½ teaspoon minced fresh thyme

· Salt and freshly ground black pepper

· Pinch sugar, optional

· 5 medium artichokes, about ½ pound each, trimmed as directed on page 37 and kept in acidulated water

· 2 tablespoons olive oil

· Salt and black pepper

· ½ cup chicken stock

· 2 large cloves garlic, minced

· 1 tablespoon olive oil

· 1 pound fresh egg pasta in sheets

· Unsalted butter, for baking dish

· ½ cup freshly grated Parmesan cheese

🍃 Bring a large pot of salted water to a boil. Fill a large bowl with ice water and stir in olive oil. If you are using store-bought fresh pasta, it is probably not thin enough. Cut the sheets into manageable widths and roll them through your own pasta machine to make them thinner (see introduction).

🍃 Boil the sheets, two at a time, for 15 seconds. Carefully transfer to the ice water and stir to make sure they do not stick to one another or themselves.

🍃 Preheat oven to 400°F. Thickly butter the bottom and sides of a 9-by-13-inch baking dish.

🍃 To assemble lasagne lift sheets of pasta out of the ice water as you need them, and pat them thoroughly dry between two dish towels. Line the bottom of the baking dish with pasta cut to fit, with no overlap. Spread one-fifth of the artichoke mixture evenly over the noodles. Top with a second layer of pasta, cut to fit. Spread another one-fifth of the artichoke mixture evenly over the noodles.

Repeat layers of pasta and artichoke mixture until you have six layers of pasta and five of artichoke. (You may not need all the pasta.) Spread tomato sauce evenly atop final layer of pasta. Sprinkle the Parmesan evenly over the top.

🍃 Bake until cheese on top has melted and is beginning to brown and lasagne is hot throughout, about 20 minutes. Let stand 10 minutes before cutting. Serve on warm dishes. Serves 6.

GEMELLI WITH ARTICHOKES, OLIVES, FETA AND CAPERS

I FIRST ENCOUNTERED THIS APPEALING COMBINATION AT OLIVETO, A DELIGHTFUL ITALIAN RESTAURANT NEAR MY OAKLAND, CALIFORNIA, HOME. THE CHEF THERE USED GEMELLI, WHICH ARE HARD TO FIND. PENNE OR FUSILLI MAKE GOOD SUBSTITUTES.

· 20 baby artichokes, 1½ to 2 ounces each, trimmed as directed on page 37 and kept in acidulated water

· 20 baby artichokes, 1½ to 2 ounces each, trimmed as directed on page 37 and kept in acidulated water

· 5 tablespoons olive oil

· 2 cloves garlic, minced

· Salt and hot red pepper flakes

· 1 pound dried gemelli ("twins"), penne rigate (ridged tubes) or fusilli

· ½ cup freshly grated Asiago cheese

· ¼ cup capers, rinsed

· 4 dozen Niçoise olives, pitted

· Generous 4 ounces Greek or Bulgarian feta cheese, crumbled

✎ Drain artichokes and chop them coarsely. I halve them lengthwise, then cut each half into neat dice by slicing two or three times in each direction.

✎ Heat 4 tablespoons of the oil in a 12-inch skillet over moderate heat. Add garlic and sauté 1 minute to release its fragrance. Add artichokes, salt and hot red pepper flakes to taste. Toss to coat with oil. Cover and reduce heat to moderately low. Cook artichokes in their own steam, uncovering and stirring occasionally to make sure they aren't sticking. They should be tender and appetizingly browned in spots in about 15 minutes. You should not need additional liquid, but you can add a tablespoon or two of water if artichokes begin to stick. When artichokes are tender, turn off heat.

✎ Cook pasta in a large pot of boiling salted water until al dente. Drain. Transfer pasta to a large warm bowl. Add remaining 1 tablespoon olive oil and ¼ cup of the Asiago cheese; toss to coat. Add artichokes, capers, olives and feta. Toss to mix well. Serve immediately on warm dishes, topping each serving with a little of the remaining Asiago. Serves 4.

CAVATAPPI WITH ARTICHOKES AND TOMATO

HERE, I STEW SLICED BABY ARTICHOKES UNTIL THEY'RE BROWNED IN SPOTS AND TENDER, THEN I STIR THEM INTO A THICK AND AROMATIC TOMATO SAUCE. I LIKE THIS METHOD BETTER THAN STEWING THEM IN THE TOMATO SAUCE; THEY GET CRISP ON THE EDGES AND THE TOMATO SAUCE STAYS SWEET INSTEAD OF ADOPTING THE SOMEWHAT BITTER FLAVOR OF THE ARTICHOKES. CAVATAPPI, ALSO CALLED TORTIGLIONE, HAVE A CORKSCREW SHAPE THAT TRAPS A SAUCE NICELY.

· *20 baby artichokes, 1½ to 2 ounces each, trimmed as directed on page 37 and kept in acidulated water*

· *2 tablespoons olive oil*

· *Salt and freshly ground black pepper*

· *1 recipe Neapolitan Tomato Sauce (page 151)*

· *1 pound dried cavatappi ("corkscrews"), farfalle ("butterflies") or penne*

· *1 cup freshly grated Parmesan cheese*

Drain artichokes, halve lengthwise and then slice lengthwise as thinly as possible.

Heat olive oil in a 12-inch skillet over moderately high heat. Add artichokes and toss to coat with oil. Season well with salt and pepper. Cover and reduce heat to cook artichokes in their own steam, uncovering and stirring occasionally to make sure they aren't sticking. They should be tender and appetizingly browned in spots in 15 to 20 minutes. You should not need additional liquid, but you can add a tablespoon or two of water if artichokes begin to stick.

Add the tomato sauce to the artichokes and stir to combine. Taste and adjust seasoning. Reheat gently, adding a few tablespoons of water if necessary to thin the sauce.

Cook pasta in a large pot of boiling salted water until al dente. Drain, reserving about ½ cup of the cooking water. Transfer pasta to a large warm bowl. Add sauce and toss, adding as much of the reserved cooking water as needed to help the sauce coat the pasta nicely. Serve immediately on warm dishes, topping each portion with a little of the Parmesan. Pass remaining Parmesan at the table. Serves 4.

FETTUCCINE WITH ARTICHOKES, PROSCIUTTO AND CREAM

FRESH FETTUCCINE IN CREAM WITH NUGGETS OF ARTICHOKE AND MINCED PROSCIUTTO IS A BEAUTIFUL DISH FOR A SPRING DINNER. FOR THE MOST SATISFYING RESULTS, DON'T REDUCE THE SAUCE TOO MUCH AFTER ADDING THE CREAM. IT SHOULD LOOK A LITTLE THIN BEFORE YOU ADD THE PASTA, BECAUSE FRESH PASTA DRINKS UP SAUCE LIKE A SPONGE. IF YOU FOLLOW THESE DIRECTIONS, YOU'LL HAVE SAUCE THAT'S JUST THE RIGHT TEXTURE TO COAT THE PASTA LIGHTLY, WITH NO PUDDLE ON THE PLATE.

· 20 baby artichokes, 1½ to 2 ounces each, trimmed as directed on page 37 and kept in acidulated water

· 2 tablespoons unsalted butter

· 2 tablespoons olive oil

· ¼ cup minced shallots

· 1 teaspoon minced fresh thyme

· Salt and freshly ground black pepper

· 1 cup heavy cream

· 1 cup chicken stock

· 2 ounces prosciutto di Parma, finely minced

· 3 tablespoons minced parsley

· 1 pound fresh fettuccine

Drain artichokes and chop them coarsely. I halve them lengthwise, then cut each half into neat dice by slicing two or three times in each direction.

Melt butter with olive oil in a 12-inch skillet over moderate heat. Add shallots and sauté until softened, about 2 minutes. Add artichokes and thyme and season well with salt and pepper. Stir to coat with fat, then cover and reduce heat to moderately low. Cook artichokes in their own steam, uncovering and stirring occasionally to make sure they aren't sticking. They should be tender and appetizingly browned in spots in about 15 minutes. You should not need additional liquid, but you can add a tablespoon or two of water if artichokes begin to stick. When artichokes are done, stir in cream and stock. Simmer briefly to reduce sauce to texture of rich cream. Stir in prosciutto and 2 tablespoons of the parsley. Taste and adjust seasoning.

Cook pasta in a large pot of boiling salted water until al dente. Just before pasta is ready, reheat sauce gently; do not allow sauce to reduce much or it will be too thick. Drain pasta, reserving about ½ cup of the cooking water. Transfer pasta to a large warm bowl. Add sauce and toss, adding some of the reserved cooking water if needed to help the sauce coat the noodles nicely. Serve immediately on warm dishes, garnishing each portion with a little of the remaining 1 tablespoon parsley. Serves 4.

SPAGHETTI WITH SHREDDED ARTICHOKES

LET THE SHREDDED ARTICHOKES BROWN A LITTLE IN THE SKILLET; THE CARAMELIZATION ADDS AN APPEALING FLAVOR AND APPETIZING COLOR TO THE FINISHED DISH.

· *20 baby artichokes, 1½ to 2 ounces each, trimmed as directed on page 37 and kept in acidulated water*

· *5 tablespoons olive oil*

· *4 large cloves garlic, minced*

· *¼ teaspoon hot red pepper flakes*

· *Salt*

· *1 pound dried spaghetti*

· *1 cup freshly grated pecorino romano cheese*

· *¼ cup minced parsley*

❧ Drain artichokes, halve lengthwise and then slice lengthwise as thinly as possible.

❧ Heat 4 tablespoons of the olive oil in a 12-inch skillet over moderately low heat. Add garlic and sauté 1 minute to release its fragrance. Add hot red pepper flakes and artichokes. Season well with salt. Toss to coat with oil. Cover and cook artichokes in their own steam, uncovering and stirring occasionally to make sure they aren't sticking. They should be tender and appetizingly browned in spots in 15 to 20 minutes. You should not need additional liquid, but you can add a tablespoon or two of water if artichokes begin to stick.

❧ Cook pasta in a large pot of boiling salted water until al dente. Drain, reserving about ½ cup of the cooking water. Transfer pasta to a large warm bowl. Add remaining 1 tablespoon olive oil and ½ cup of the cheese; toss to coat. Add contents of skillet, remaining ½ cup cheese and parsley and toss again, adding a little reserved cooking water if needed to make noodles glisten. If you have some nice browned bits stuck to the skillet, release them by adding a few tablespoons of hot pasta water and stirring with a wooden spoon; then add those flavorful juices to the pasta. Serve immediately on warm dishes. Serves 4.

ASPARAGUS

ASPARAGUS BECAUSE FRESH ASPARAGUS SPEARS COOK SO QUICKLY, THEY CAN BE THE FOUNDATION OF SOME PARTICULARLY FAST PASTA SAUCES. IN FACT, DITALI WITH ASPARAGUS (PAGE 48) IS PROBABLY THE EASIEST AND MOST QUICKLY MADE DISH IN THIS BOOK. *0* THE DOMESTIC ASPARAGUS SEASON RUNS FROM MID-FEBRUARY TO JUNE, WITH PEAK SUPPLIES FROM MARCH THROUGH MAY. SPEARS CAN RANGE IN THICKNESS FROM WISPY THIN TO JUMBO. SOME PASTA SAUCES WORK BEST WITH THIN ONES; OTHERS REQUIRE A THICKER SPEAR. FOR EACH OF THE FOLLOWING RECIPES, I HAVE SPECIFIED THE MOST APPROPRIATE SIZE. *0* AT THE MARKET, LOOK FOR FIRM GREEN SPEARS WITH TIGHTLY CLOSED TIPS AND MOIST ENDS. AVOID LIMP ONES OR ANY THAT LOOK WOODY OR DRIED OUT. GOOD PRODUCE MANAGERS KEEP THEIR ASPARAGUS SPEARS BUTT END DOWN IN A LITTLE WATER. IF YOU CAN'T USE THEM THE DAY YOU BUY THEM, WRAP THE BUTT ENDS IN DAMP PAPER TOWELS AND STORE THE SPEARS IN A PLASTIC BAG IN THE REFRIGERATOR CRISPER.

LINGUINE WITH ASPARAGUS AND EGG   ✓ 9-20

EGG "COOKED" IN THE HEAT OF HOT PASTA MAKES A CREAMY SAUCE THAT HELPS BIND THE ASPARAGUS AND CHEESE TO THE NOODLES. IF YOU'VE EVER HAD SPAGHETTI CARBONARA, WITH PANCETTA AND EGG, YOU KNOW HOW DELICIOUS SUCH A PREPARATION CAN BE. THINK OF THIS DISH AS A "VEGETARIAN CARBONARA" THAT TAKES ADVANTAGE OF THE GREAT AFFINITY OF ASPARAGUS AND EGGS.

I LIKE COARSELY CRACKED BLACK PEPPER IN THIS DISH (CRACKED WITH A MORTAR AND PESTLE) BUT FRESHLY GROUND PEPPER WILL DO. USE A LOT OF IT.

· 2 pounds asparagus spears, preferably thin

· 4 eggs

· ¼ cup heavy cream

· ¾ cup freshly grated Parmesan cheese

· Salt and freshly cracked black pepper

0 Holding an asparagus spear in both hands, bend it gently; it will break naturally at point at which spear becomes tough. Repeat with remaining spears. Discard tough ends. Cut spears on the diagonal into pieces about ⅓ inch wide. (Line several spears up and cut across them all at once to save time.)

0 Whisk eggs and cream together in a bowl. Stir in cheese and a generous quantity of salt and pepper. Set aside.

0 Heat olive oil and butter in a 12-inch skillet over moderately low heat. Add onion and sauté until soft and sweet, 10 to 15 minutes.

- *1 tablespoon olive oil*
- *1 tablespoon unsalted butter*
- *1 medium yellow onion, minced*
- *1 pound dried linguine or spaghetti*

Meanwhile, bring a large pot of salted water to a boil. Add asparagus and boil until tender, 5 to 8 minutes. Lift them out with a skimmer and add to skillet. Season generously with salt and pepper; toss or stir to coat with onions and fat. Keep hot while you cook the pasta.

Boil pasta until al dente in the same water you used to cook the asparagus. Drain, reserving about 1 cup of the cook-ing water. Immediately return pasta to the hot pot off the heat. Add egg mixture and stir briskly to coat all the noodles with the sauce; the hot pasta will "cook" the egg. Add asparagus and onions and toss again, adding as much of the reserved cooking water as needed to moisten the noodles. Serve immediately on warm dishes. Serves 4.

PASTA "RISOTTO" WITH ASPARAGUS

ROSMARINO PASTA LOOKS LIKE LONG-GRAIN RICE. IN FACT, IF YOU COOK IT LIKE RISOTTO—SIMMERING IT IN A SMALL AMOUNT OF STOCK IN AN OPEN POT AND STIRRING OFTEN—IT WILL PLUMP UP AND GET CREAMY IN THE SAME WAY THAT ARBORIO RICE DOES. I HAVE FOUND THAT IT DOESN'T MAKE MUCH DIFFERENCE WHETHER YOU ADD THE HOT STOCK A LITTLE AT A TIME, AS FOR RISOTTO (SEE PASTA "RISOTTO" WITH MUSHROOMS AND FONTINA, PAGE 100), OR ALL AT ONCE, AS I DO HERE. IT IS IMPORTANT, HOWEVER, TO ADJUST THE HEAT SO THAT THE LIQUID IS ABSORBED BY THE TIME THE PASTA IS COOKED, IN 10 TO 11 MINUTES. THIS IS AN UNCONVENTIONAL METHOD FOR COOKING PASTA, BUT IT'S DELICIOUS; ON ANOTHER NIGHT, TRY PEAS, FAVA BEANS OR CHOPPED BROCCOLI IN PLACE OF THE ASPARAGUS. IF YOU CAN'T FIND ROSMARINO, USE ORZO, WHICH IS ABOUT THE SAME SIZE.

- *2 pounds medium asparagus*
- *4 tablespoons unsalted butter*
- *2 large shallots, minced*
- *Salt and freshly ground black pepper*
- *Approximately 5 cups hot chicken stock*
- *1 pound dried rosmarino or orzo pasta*
- *2/3 cup freshly grated Parmesan cheese, plus additional Parmesan cheese for passing*

Holding an asparagus spear in both hands, bend it gently; it will break naturally at point at which spear becomes tough. Repeat with remaining spears. Discard tough ends. Cut spears crosswise into pieces 1/3 inch wide. (Line several spears up and cut across them all at once to save time.)

Melt butter in a 6- to 8-quart pot over moderate heat. Add shallots and sauté until softened, about 2 minutes. Add asparagus and stir to coat with butter. Season with salt and pepper. Add 2 cups of the hot stock, bring to a simmer, cover and reduce heat to maintain a simmer. Cook until tender, 8 to 10 minutes. →

Uncover and stir in pasta. Add 2½ cups more of the hot stock. Bring to a simmer, adjust heat to maintain a simmer and cook, stirring frequently, until pasta is al dente and all the liquid has been absorbed, about 10 minutes. You may or may not need the remaining ½ cup stock, depending on the size and shape of your pan and the heat of your stove. Add it if the dish looks too dry; the finished dish should be as creamy as a risotto.

When pasta is barely tender, remove from heat, cover and let stand 3 minutes. Stir in ⅔ cup Parmesan, adjust seasoning and serve in warm bowls. Pass additional Parmesan at the table. Serves 4.

DITALI WITH ASPARAGUS

DITALI ARE HOLLOW TUBES ABOUT ⅓ INCH LONG AND EQUALLY WIDE. CANNERONI IS ANOTHER NAME FOR A SIMILAR SHAPE. MOST PEOPLE USE DITALI IN SOUP, BUT I LOVE THEM IN THIS DISH, WHERE THEY MIMIC THE SHAPE OF THE SLICED ASPARAGUS. YOU MAY HAVE TO SEARCH FOR DITALI, BUT THAT WILL BE THE HARDEST PART OF THIS SIMPLE RECIPE.

THIS IS A ONE-POT DISH: THE PASTA AND VEGETABLE COOK TOGETHER AND ARE SAUCED IN THE SERVING BOWL. IT IS SO MILD AND FUN TO EAT THAT CHILDREN WILL LOVE IT.

· 2½ to 3 pounds thick asparagus spears

· 1 pound dried ditali ("thimbles") or canneroni

· 4 tablespoons unsalted butter, in pieces

· 1 cup freshly grated Parmesan cheese

· Salt and freshly ground black pepper

The amount of asparagus to buy depends on how well trimmed they are when you buy them. Holding an asparagus spear in both hands, bend it gently; it will break naturally at point at which spear becomes tough. Repeat with remaining spears. Discard tough ends. You should have about 1½ pounds tender spears. Cut spears crosswise into slices ⅓ inch thick, about the same length as the ditali. (Line several spears up and cut across them all at once to save time.)

Bring a large pot of salted water to a boil. Add asparagus and cover the pot partially. When water returns to a boil, add ditali. Cook until pasta is al dente. Drain pasta and asparagus. Transfer to a large warm bowl. Add butter, cheese and salt and pepper to taste. Toss to coat. Serve immediately on warm dishes. Serves 4.

BEANS / BROCCOLI

FAVA BEANS / GREEN BEANS

· Conchiglie with Fava Beans, Tomato and Pecorino

· Fettuccine with Fava Beans, Saffron and Cream

· Fettuccine with Braised Green Beans

· Orecchiette with Fava Beans and Prosciutto

BROCCOLI / BROCCOLI RABE

· Orecchiette with White Beans and Broccoli Rabe

· Fusilli with Broccoli Sauce

· Orecchiette with Broccoli

· Spaghetti with Broccoli Rabe, Olives and Provolone

FAVA BEANS / GREEN BEANS

FAVA BEANS (ALSO KNOWN AS BROAD BEANS) SHOW UP IN MY NEIGHBORHOOD PRODUCE MARKETS IN MID- TO LATE SPRING AND AGAIN IN THE FALL. THEY LOOK A LITTLE LIKE OVERGROWN GREEN BEANS, WHICH MAY BE WHY THEY'RE ALSO SOMETIMES CALLED "HORSE BEANS." THE THICK, GREEN POD IS NOT EDIBLE, BUT SLIT IT OPEN AND YOU'LL FIND SEVERAL KIDNEY-SHAPED BEANS NESTLING IN A FUZZY BED. THE BEANS THEMSELVES NEED TO BE PEELED, BUT THAT'S EASILY DONE IF YOU BLANCH THEM FIRST. SHELLING AND PEELING FAVA BEANS CAN BE TEDIOUS, BUT I ACTUALLY DON'T MIND IT. I POUR A GLASS OF WINE FOR MYSELF AND MY HUSBAND AND WE PEEL THEM TOGETHER, TALKING OVER THE EVENTS OF THE DAY. ∅ AT THE MARKET, LOOK FOR FAVAS THAT HAVE A VELVETY FEEL, WITH FEW BLEMISHES. YOU SHOULD BE ABLE TO FEEL THE BEANS DEVELOPED INSIDE, BUT CHOOSE SMALLER PODS OVER LARGER ONES. ∅ YOU MAY NEVER HAVE CONSIDERED GREEN BEANS AS THE BASIS FOR A PASTA SAUCE, BUT I HOPE YOU WILL NOW. IF THEY ARE COOKED UNTIL SOFT AND SWEET (FORGET AL DENTE) THEY MAKE A WONDERFUL PASTA SAUCE. PLEASE MAKE IT ONLY WHEN YOU CAN FIND YOUNG, SLENDER BEANS—PROBABLY IN EARLY TO MID-SUMMER.

CONCHIGLIE WITH FAVA BEANS, TOMATO AND PECORINO

IN ITALY, WHEN FAVA BEANS ARE IN SEASON, PEOPLE EAT THEM RAW AS AN HORS D'OEUVRE WITH CUBES OF YOUNG PECORINO CHEESE. THIS PASTA SAUCE BUILDS ON THAT IDEA, WITH A LITTLE FRESH TOMATO ADDED TO CREATE A LIGHT SAUCE. YOU WILL NEED A YOUNG SHEEP'S MILK CHEESE THAT'S FIRM ENOUGH TO GRATE. ITALIAN TOSCANELLO OR SPANISH MANCHEGO IS A GOOD CHOICE.

CONCHIGLIE RIGATE ARE RIDGED PASTA SHELLS ABOUT 1 INCH LONG. THEY ARE PARTICULARLY GOOD WITH CHUNKY VEGETABLE SAUCES SUCH AS THIS ONE, BECAUSE THE VEGETABLES CAN SLIP INTO THE HOLLOWS.

· 4 pounds fava beans

· ¼ cup olive oil

· 2 cups peeled, seeded and chopped tomatoes (page 22)

· 1 cup minced green onions (scallions), white and pale green parts only

· 1 teaspoon minced fresh thyme

· Salt and freshly ground black pepper →

∅ Remove fava beans from their fuzzy pods. To peel individual beans, bring a large pot of water—at least 5 quarts—to a boil over high heat. Add the favas and blanch about 30 seconds if they are small, up to 1 minute if they are large, and then lift them out with a skimmer. While they are hot, pinch open the end of the bean opposite the end that connected it to the pod. The peeled bean will slip out easily. Reserve cooking water. →

- 1 pound dried conchiglie rigate ("ridged shells") or gemelli ("twins")
- 1½ cups freshly grated young sheep's milk (see introduction)
- ½ cup freshly grated pecorino romano cheese

In a 12-inch skillet, combine olive oil, tomatoes, green onions, thyme, and salt and pepper to taste. Bring to a simmer over moderate heat, adjust heat to maintain a simmer and cook, stirring occasionally, until reduced to a thick sauce, about 15 minutes. Add a little water if necessary to keep the sauce from sticking.

Add salt to reserved cooking water and bring to a boil. Add fava beans and boil until tender, a minute or two if they are small. Lift out with a skimmer and add to tomato sauce. Stir to coat; taste and adjust seasoning.

Cook pasta in the same boiling water until al dente. Drain and transfer to a large warm bowl. Add sauce and toss; add young sheep's milk cheese and toss. Serve immediately on warm dishes. Top each serving with 2 tablespoons pecorino romano. Serves 4.

FETTUCCINE WITH FAVA BEANS, SAFFRON AND CREAM

TAKE CARE NOT TO REDUCE THE CREAM MIXTURE TOO MUCH; FRESH PASTA DRINKS UP A LOT OF SAUCE. YOU WANT ENOUGH TO COAT THE NOODLES LIGHTLY, WITH NO PUDDLE LEFT ON THE PLATE. IF YOU DO FIND YOU HAVE TOO LITTLE SAUCE, ADD A LITTLE HOT PASTA WATER TO THIN IT OUT.

- 4 pounds fava beans
- 2 tablespoons unsalted butter
- 1 cup chopped green onions (scallions), white and pale green parts only
- 1 cup chicken stock
- ¼ teaspoon loosely packed saffron threads (about 30 threads)
- ¾ cup heavy cream
- ¼ cup minced parsley
- Salt and freshly ground black pepper
- 1 pound fresh fettuccine

Remove fava beans from their fuzzy pods. To peel individual beans, bring a large pot of water — at least 5 quarts — to a boil over high heat. Add the favas and blanch about 30 seconds if they are small, up to 1 minute if they are large, and then lift them out with a skimmer. While they are hot, pinch open the end of the bean opposite the end that connected it to the pod. The peeled bean will slip out easily. Reserve cooking water.

Heat butter in a 12-inch skillet over moderately low heat. Add green onions and sauté until softened and fragrant, about 1 minute. Add favas and stir to coat with onions and butter. Add chicken stock and saffron; cover and simmer until favas are crisp-tender, about 3 minutes. Uncover and stir in cream and all but ½ tablespoon of the parsley. Season to taste with salt and pepper. Set aside.

Add salt to water used to blanch fava beans, bring to a boil, add pasta and cook until al dente. Just before pasta is ready, reheat fava beans gently; do not allow the sauce to reduce much or it will be too thick. Drain pasta, reserving about ½ cup of the cooking water. Transfer pasta to a large warm bowl. Add contents of skillet and toss to coat with sauce, adding some of the reserved cooking water if needed to help the sauce coat the noodles nicely. Serve immediately on warm dishes. Top each serving with a little of the remaining parsley. Serves 4.

FETTUCCINE WITH BRAISED GREEN BEANS

- 1½ pounds young, slender green beans (see introduction), ends trimmed
- 1½ cups peeled, seeded and chopped fresh tomatoes (page 22) or strained canned tomatoes (pages 21–22)
- ¼ cup olive oil
- 6 cloves garlic, minced
- ½ teaspoon fennel seed, lightly crushed in a mortar or spice grinder
- ¼ teaspoon hot red pepper flakes
- Salt
- Approximately 4 cups chicken stock, vegetable stock or water
- 1 pound fresh fettuccine
- 1 cup freshly grated Parmesan cheese

MY FRIEND ENZO POLACCO SHOWED ME HOW DELICIOUS GREEN BEANS COULD BE WHEN COOKED SLOWLY FOR A LONG TIME. THEY GET SOFT AND SWEET AND SILKY, AND HAVE AN INTENSE BEAN FLAVOR. HE SERVED THEM TO ME AS A SIDE DISH, BUT I ASKED HIM LATER HOW HE THOUGHT THEY WOULD WORK AS A PASTA SAUCE. "FINE," HE SAID, ADDING WITH TYPICAL ITALIAN CONVICTION, "BUT ONLY WITH FRESH PASTA!"

BESIDES THE FRESH PASTA, YOU WILL NEED YOUNG, SLENDER GREEN BEANS—THE KIND THE FRENCH CALL *HARICOTS VERTS*. VERY YOUNG BLUE LAKE BEANS WILL WORK, TOO. THEY SHOULD BE NO BIGGER AROUND THAN A PENCIL.

In a 12-inch skillet, combine beans, tomatoes, olive oil, garlic, fennel seed, hot red pepper flakes and salt to taste. Add enough stock or water to come just to the top of the beans, about 4 cups. Bring to a simmer. Cover partially, reduce heat to maintain a simmer and cook until beans are very tender—soft enough to twirl in a fork with fettuccine. Depending on the size and age of the beans, it will take 1½ to 2 hours. Check occasionally to make sure liquid has not evaporated; add a little more stock or water if beans seem too dry. At the end of the cooking time, there should be just a few table-spoons of unabsorbed liquid, enough to coat noodles nicely. If necessary, cook the beans uncovered during the last few min-utes to evaporate excess liquid.

Cook pasta in a large pot of boiling salted water until al dente. Drain and transfer to a large warm bowl. Add beans and toss to coat. Add Parmesan and toss again. Serve immediately on warm dishes. Serves 4.

ORECCHIETTE WITH FAVA BEANS AND PROSCIUTTO

FAVA BEANS ARE SO SWEET AND DELICATE IN THE SPRING THAT I DON'T LIKE TO COVER THEM UP WITH BOLD FLAVORS. A LITTLE MILD GREEN ONION AND A BIT OF MINCED ITALIAN HAM ARE PERFECT COMPLEMENTS. ORECCHIETTE HAVE A TENDENCY TO STICK TOGETHER IN THE PASTA POT; STIRRING OFTEN WITH A WOODEN SPOON WHILE THEY COOK HELPS TO KEEP THEM SEPARATE.

· 4 pounds fava beans

· 2 tablespoons unsalted butter

· 2 tablespoons olive oil

· 2 bunches green onions (scallions), white and pale green parts only, minced

· Salt and freshly ground black pepper

· 1 pound dried orecchiette ("little ears") or gnocchi

· 3 ounces prosciutto di Parma, minced

· 1 cup freshly grated pecorino romano cheese

Remove fava beans from their fuzzy pods. To peel individual beans, bring a large pot of water—at least 5 quarts—to a boil over high heat. Add the favas and cook until the bright green beans inside are just tender, about 2 to 4 minutes depending on size; lift one out and pinch it open to test. Transfer with a skimmer to a bowl of ice water. Pinch open the end of the bean opposite the end that connected it to the pod. The peeled bean will slip out easily. Reserve cooking water.

Heat butter and oil in a 12-inch skillet over moderately low heat. Add green onions and cook until softened and fragrant, about 3 minutes. Add fava beans and toss to coat with onions and fat. Season well with salt and pepper. Add ½ cup water, bring to a simmer and keep warm.

Add salt to water used to blanch fava beans, bring to a boil, add pasta and cook until al dente, stirring often to keep orecchiette from sticking together. Just before pasta is ready, add prosciutto to fava beans. Drain pasta, reserving about ½ cup of the cooking water. Transfer pasta to a large warm bowl. Add contents of skillet and toss to coat. Add cheese and toss again, adding some of the reserved cooking water if needed to moisten the dish. Serve immediately on warm dishes. Serves 4.

BROCCOLI / BROCCOLI RABE

NO AMERICAN NEEDS AN INTRODUCTION TO BROCCOLI BUT MANY DON'T KNOW BROCCOLI RABE. THIS DEEP GREEN LEAFY VEGETABLE GOES BY MANY NAMES—RAPE, *RAPINI*, BROCCOLI RAAB, *BROCOLETTI DI RAPE* AND *CIMA DI RAPA* AMONG THEM— AND FOR YEARS HAS BEEN APPRECIATED IN THIS COUNTRY PRIMARILY BY ITALIAN-AMERICANS. IT IS RAPIDLY BECOMING MORE WIDELY AVAILABLE, HOWEVER, WHICH IS GOOD NEWS BECAUSE IT'S HIGHLY NUTRITIOUS, DISTINCTLY FLAVORED AND DELICIOUS WITH PASTA. ❂ BROCCOLI RABE LOOKS LIKE NONHEADING BROCCOLI, WITH THIN STEMS, ABUNDANT LEAVES AND SMALL FLORETS. SOMETIMES A FEW OF THE FLORETS HAVE BLOSSOMED INTO BRIGHT YELLOW FLOWERS. IT IS MORE ASSERTIVE IN TASTE THAN BROC- COLI, WITH A BITTER EDGE THAT I LOVE. A COOL-WEATHER CROP, IT IS EASIEST TO FIND IN FALL, WINTER AND SPRING. CHOOSE BROCCOLI RABE WITH THIN STEMS, HEALTHY-LOOKING LEAVES AND FEW YELLOW FLOWERS. BEFORE COOKING, REMOVE ANY THICK STEMS; LEAVE THE THIN, MORE TENDER STEMS ATTACHED. ❂ FOR CONVENTIONAL BROCCOLI, LOOK FOR STEMS ON THE THIN SIDE (THICK ONES CAN BE WOODY) AND TIGHTLY CLOSED FLORETS WITH NO YELLOWING. ❂ IN LIGHT OF THE NUTRITIONAL PROFILE OF BROCCOLI AND BROCCOLI RABE—BOTH ARE LOW IN CALORIES, HIGH IN VITAMINS A AND C, AND GOOD SOURCES OF FIBER—IT SEEMS TO ME THAT A DINNER OF PASTA WITH BROCCOLI IS ONE OF THE MOST SENSIBLE THINGS YOU CAN EAT.

ORECCHIETTE WITH WHITE BEANS AND BROCCOLI RABE

I USE CANNELLINI BEANS OR GREAT NORTHERN BEANS HERE, BUT USE WHATEVER YOU LIKE: DRIED CRANBERRY BEANS, FAVA BEANS OR EVEN LIMA BEANS OR FRENCH FLAGEOLETS WOULD BE APPEALING. YOU CAN ALSO USE RINSED AND DRAINED CANNED BEANS, ALTHOUGH THEN YOU WON'T HAVE A FLAVORFUL BROTH FOR THINNING THE SAUCE. USE A LITTLE HOT PASTA WATER INSTEAD.

PASS EXTRA VIRGIN OLIVE OIL AT THE TABLE FOR THOSE WHO MIGHT WANT TO DRIZZLE A LITTLE ON TOP.

· ⅔ cup dried white beans

· ½ yellow onion, peeled and halved

· 3 cloves garlic, halved, plus 3 large cloves garlic, minced

❂ Soak beans overnight in water to cover; drain. Place them in a saucepan with water to cover by 1 inch. Bring to a boil slowly, skimming any white foam that collects on the surface. Add onion, halved garlic cloves and bay leaf. Cover partially, adjust heat to maintain a simmer and cook until beans are tender, about 1 hour. Discard onion, garlic and bay leaf. Season with salt and pepper; let cool.

- *1 bay leaf*
- *Salt and freshly ground black pepper*
- *3 to 4 ounces pancetta, minced*
- *1 tablespoon olive oil*
- *Scant ½ teaspoon minced fresh rosemary*
- *1 pound broccoli rabe*
- *1 pound dried orecchiette ("little ears")*
- *⅔ cup freshly grated pecorino romano cheese*

Combine pancetta and olive oil in a 12-inch skillet. Cook over moderately low heat, stirring occasionally, until pancetta begins to crisp, 3 to 5 minutes. Do not allow it to brown. Stir in minced garlic and rosemary. Sauté 1 minute to release garlic fragrance. Drain beans, reserving their liquid, and add them to the skillet. Stir gently to coat with fat and seasonings. Set aside.

Bring a large pot of salted water — at least 5 quarts — to a boil. Meanwhile, trim broccoli rabe, cutting away thick tough stems but leaving tender stems attached; you want to have about ¾ pound after trimming. Add broccoli rabe to the boiling water and cook until stems are just tender, about 2 minutes. Lift out with tongs and place in a bowl of ice water to stop the cooking. Reserve cooking water. Drain broccoli well, then squeeze gently between your hands to remove excess water. Chop the stems into ¼-inch lengths; chop the florets and leaves coarsely. Add to skillet and toss gently to coat. Season with salt and pepper. Remove from heat until pasta is ready.

Boil pasta until al dente in the same water you used to cook the broccoli. Just before pasta is ready, reheat beans and broccoli, adding a few tablespoons of bean broth if necessary to keep mixture from sticking. Drain pasta and transfer to a large warm bowl. Add contents of skillet and toss. Add cheese and toss again. Serve immediately on warm dishes. Serves 4.

FUSILLI WITH BROCCOLI SAUCE

I LOVE THE WAY THIS CREAMY SAUCE SLIPS INTO THE CORKSCREWLIKE GROOVES OF FUSILLI; THIS IS TRULY AN IDEAL MARRIAGE OF SHAPE AND SAUCE.

- 4 tablespoons unsalted butter
- ¼ cup minced shallots
- Approximately 1½ pounds broccoli
- ½ cup chicken stock
- ½ cup heavy cream
- Salt and freshly ground black pepper
- 1 pound dried fusilli
- ¼ cup freshly grated Parmesan cheese, plus additional Parmesan cheese for passing

Melt 2 tablespoons of the butter in a 10-inch skillet over moderately low heat. Add shallots and saute until soft and sweet, about 5 minutes. Set aside.

Bring a large pot of salted water — at least 5 quarts — to a boil. Meanwhile, separate broccoli florets from stems, but keep florets in large pieces. If stem ends are thick and woody, cut them off and discard them. With a vegetable peeler or small, sharp knife, peel the stems down to the pale green heart. You should have about 1 pound florets and peeled stems.

Add florets and stems to boiling water and cook until just tender. The florets will cook in 2 to 3 minutes; the stems will take 3 to 4 minutes longer. Lift out with tongs or a skimmer and drain well, then transfer to a food processor fitted with the steel blade. (Do not discard broccoli cooking water.) Add shallots and any butter in skillet. Process well, stopping to scrape down sides of bowl a few times. Add chicken stock and process again until as smooth as possible. (It will not be completely smooth.) Transfer mixture to a 10-inch skillet and stir in cream. Season

highly with salt and pepper. Just before you need it, reheat sauce gently over low heat. Do not cook too long or the sauce will start to lose its pretty green color.

Boil pasta until al dente in the same water you used to cook the broccoli. Drain, reserving about ½ cup of the cooking water. Transfer pasta to a large warm bowl. Add remaining 2 table-spoons butter and toss to melt butter. Add sauce (you may not need all of it; use as much as you like) and toss again, adding a little of the cooking water if needed to thin the sauce. Serve immediately on warm dishes. Top each serving with 1 tablespoon of grated Parmesan and pass additional Parmesan at the table. Serves 4.

ORECCHIETTE WITH BROCCOLI

A LOT OF PEOPLE THINK THE FLORETS ARE THE CHOICE PART OF BROCCOLI, BUT I DISAGREE. IF THE BROCCOLI ISN'T OLD AND OVERGROWN, THE STEMS ARE DELICIOUS: THEY JUST NEED TO BE PEELED TO REMOVE THE TOUGH SKIN. THE TENDER STEMS OF YOUNG BROCCOLI DON'T EVEN NEED PEELING. COOK THEM WITH THE FLORETS AND CHOP THEM TOGETHER TO MAKE A QUICK, HEALTHFUL AND ECONOMICAL PASTA TOPPING.

I LIKE THIS SAUCE BEST WITH ORECCHIETTE. IF YOU CAN FIND BROCCOLI RABE, YOU CAN USE IT IN PLACE OF THE BROCCOLI. ITS STEMS ARE THINNER THAN BROCCOLI STEMS AND GENERALLY DON'T NEED PEELING, BUT YOU SHOULD REMOVE ANY THICK ONES. YOU COULD ALSO USE CAULIFLOWER IN THIS DISH, OR A COMBINATION OF BROCCOLI AND CAULIFLOWER.

- *Approximately 2 pounds broccoli*
- *5 tablespoons olive oil*
- *4 large cloves garlic, finely minced*
- *8 anchovy fillets, finely minced*
- *¼ teaspoon hot red pepper flakes*
- *Salt*
- *1 pound dried orecchiette ("little ears")*
- *1 cup freshly grated pecorino romano cheese*

⌀ Bring a large pot of salted water—at least 5 quarts—to a boil over high heat. Meanwhile, separate broccoli florets from stems, but keep florets in large clumps. If stem ends are thick and woody, cut them off and discard them. With a vegetable peeler or a small sharp knife, peel the stems down to the pale green heart. You should have about 1½ pounds florets and peeled stems.

⌀ Add stems and florets to boiling water and cook until just tender. The florets will cook in 2 to 3 minutes; the stems will take 3 to 4 minutes longer. Lift them out with tongs or a skimmer as they are done and place them in a bowl of ice water to stop the cooking. Drain stems and florets well. Chop florets coarsely; cut stems in neat ¼-inch dice. Reserve cooking water.

⌀ Heat 3 tablespoons of the olive oil in a 12-inch skillet over moderately low heat. Add garlic and sauté 1 minute to release its fragrance. Add anchovies and stir with a wooden spoon to blend with the oil. Add hot red pepper flakes. Add broccoli and stir to coat with oil and seasonings. Season well with salt. Keep warm.

⌀ Boil pasta until al dente in the same water you used to cook the broccoli, stirring often to keep orecchiette from sticking together. Drain, reserving about ½ cup of the cooking water. Transfer pasta to a large warm bowl. Add remaining 2 tablespoons oil and ½ cup of the cheese and toss. Add contents of skillet and remaining ½ cup cheese and toss again, adding a little of the reserved cooking water if needed to moisten the pasta. Serve immediately on warm dishes. Serves 4.

SPAGHETTI WITH BROCCOLI RABE, OLIVES AND PROVOLONE

AGED ITALIAN PROVOLONE TASTES SHARP ON ITS OWN, BUT ITS FLAVOR MELLOWS WHEN THE CHEESE MELTS INTO HOT PASTA. I LIKE THE PIQUANT ACCENT IT CONTRIBUTES TO THIS SIMPLE BROCCOLI SAUCE, BUT YOU CAN SUBSTITUTE PECORINO ROMANO IF YOU CAN'T FIND IMPORTED PROVOLONE. SMOKED PROVOLONE IS NOT A GOOD CHOICE. YOU CAN ALSO SUBSTITUTE BROCCOLI FOR BROCCOLI RABE. IF YOU DO, SEPARATE STEMS FROM FLORETS AND PEEL STEMS BEFORE BLANCHING. THE FLORETS WILL COOK FASTER THAN THE STEMS.

- *1½ pounds broccoli rabe*
- *¼ cup extra virgin olive oil*
- *4 cloves garlic, minced*
- *Salt and freshly ground black pepper*
- *32 dry-cured black olives, pitted and chopped*
- *1 pound dried spaghetti*
- *1 cup freshly grated Italian aged provolone cheese, plus additional provolone cheese for passing*

⌀ Bring a large pot of salted water—at least 5 quarts—to a boil. Meanwhile, trim broccoli rabe, cutting away thick, tough stems but leaving tender stems attached; you want to have 1 to 1¼ pounds after trimming. Add broccoli rabe to the boiling water and cook until stems are just tender, about 2 minutes. Lift out with tongs and place in a bowl of ice water to stop the cooking. Reserve cooking water. Drain broccoli well, then squeeze gently between your hands to remove excess water. Line up a few of the stalks at a time, stem ends together, and chop crosswise at ¼-inch intervals.

⌀ Heat olive oil in a 12-inch skillet over moderately low heat. Add garlic and sauté 1 minute to release its fragrance. Add chopped broccoli and salt and pepper to taste. Toss to coat with seasonings. Raise heat to moderate and cook just until broccoli is hot again; don't cook too long or you will lose the bright green color. Stir in olives. Keep warm.

⌀ Boil pasta until al dente in the same water you used to cook the broccoli. Drain, reserving about ½ cup of the cooking water. Transfer pasta to a large warm bowl. Add contents of skillet and toss. Add the 1 cup cheese and toss again, adding a little of the reserved cooking water if needed to moisten the dish. Serve immediately on warm dishes. Pass additional cheese at the table. Serves 4.

C

CABBAGE / CAULIFLOWER
CHARD

CABBAGE

· Fusilli with Cabbage and Tomato

· Buckwheat Pappardelle with Cabbage,
Fontina and Sage

CAULIFLOWER

· Perciatelli with Cauliflower, Tomato,
Sausage and Pine Nuts

· Orecchiette with Cauliflower

· Penne with Cauliflower Sauce

· Linguine with Cauliflower, Tomato
and Olives

CHARD

· Spaghetti with Chard, Onions and
Anchovy Butter

· Spaghetti with Chard Ribs and
Pancetta

· Gemelli with Tomato Sauce,
Chick-peas and Chard

CABBAGE

IN WINTER, WHEN PRODUCE CHOICES CAN SEEM LIMITED, CABBAGE COMES TO THE RESCUE. WHETHER SIMMERED IN A CHUNKY TOMATO SAUCE OR BRAISED IN BUTTER WITH ONIONS AND FENNEL SEED, IT MAKES AN APPEALING COLD-WEATHER PASTA SAUCE. GREEN CABBAGE SHOULD BE FIRM AND FEEL HEAVY FOR ITS SIZE. SAVOY CABBAGE, A HEADING TYPE OF GREEN CABBAGE, HAS CRINKLY LEAVES AND A MILD TASTE. IT TOO SHOULD BE FIRM AND HEAVY. BOTH TYPES OF CABBAGE ARE AVAILABLE IN GOOD SUPPLY AND QUALITY YEAR-ROUND.

FUSILLI WITH CABBAGE AND TOMATO

CABBAGE, BRAISED SLOWLY, COOKS DOWN TO SOFT SWEETNESS. HERE, IT'S SIMMERED IN TOMATO SAUCE ENRICHED WITH FINELY DICED VEGETABLES AND HERBS. THE RESULT IS A HEARTY AND HEALTHFUL DISH, A NICE MATCH FOR A ZINFANDEL OR ANOTHER LIGHT AND FRUITY RED WINE.

· ¼ cup olive oil

· 1 medium yellow onion, minced

· ⅔ cup minced carrot

· ⅔ cup minced celery

· 4 cloves garlic, minced

· ¼ teaspoon hot red pepper flakes

· 2 cups strained canned tomatoes (pages 21–22)

· 1 cup chicken stock

· 1½ tablespoons minced fresh oregano

· Salt

· Pinch sugar, optional

· ¾ pound green cabbage, cored and thinly sliced

· 1 pound dried fusilli or spaghetti

· 4 tablespoons minced parsley

· ¾ cup freshly grated Parmesan cheese

Heat olive oil in a 12-inch skillet over moderate heat. Add onion, carrot and celery and sauté until vegetables are soft and sweet, about 15 minutes. Add garlic and sauté 1 minute to release its fragrance. Add hot red pepper flakes, strained tomatoes, stock and oregano. Bring to a simmer. Taste and season with salt and with a pinch sugar if tomatoes seem a bit tart. Simmer until thick and tasty, about 15 minutes.

Add cabbage and stir to coat with sauce. Cover and simmer until cabbage is quite tender, 20 to 25 minutes. Add a little water if needed to keep sauce from sticking. Keep warm.

Cook pasta in a large pot of boiling salted water until al dente. Drain, reserving about ½ cup of the cooking water. Transfer pasta to a large warm bowl. Add sauce and 3 tablespoons of the parsley and toss to coat. Add ½ cup of the cheese and toss again, thinning the sauce if necessary with some of the reserved cooking water. Serve immediately on warm dishes, topping each serving with some of the remaining ¼ cup Parmesan and 1 tablespoon parsley. Serves 4.

BUCKWHEAT PAPPARDELLE WITH CABBAGE, FONTINA AND SAGE

SOME ITALIAN MARKETS NOW SELL DRIED PIZZOCCHERI, THE WIDE BUCKWHEAT NOODLES USED
TO MAKE A DISH OF THE SAME NAME—A LAYERING OF NOODLES, CABBAGE, POTATOES, GREEN
BEANS AND A SOFT MELTING CHEESE THAT IS A SPECIALTY OF THE VALTELLINA REGION OF
NORTHEASTERN ITALY. YOU CAN USE THOSE PACKAGED NOODLES FOR THE FOLLOWING RECIPE—
WHICH IS A SORT OF STREAMLINED PIZZOCCHERI—BUT IT'S FUN TO MAKE YOUR OWN. BECAUSE
BUCKWHEAT IS LOW IN THE PROTEINS THAT FORM GLUTEN, BUCKWHEAT DOUGH IS SOFT AND
EASY TO WORK. THE COOKED NOODLES HAVE AN EARTHY TASTE THAT IS VERY SATISFYING.

For the buckwheat pappardelle:

- *2 cups unbleached all-purpose flour*
- *1 cup buckwheat flour*
- *Large pinch salt*
- *4 eggs, beaten*
- *2 tablespoons olive oil*

For the sauce:

- *2 tablespoons unsalted butter*
- *2 tablespoons olive oil*
- *30 large fresh sage leaves*
- *2 cups sliced leeks, white and pale green parts only*
- *Salt and freshly ground black pepper*
- *1 to 1¼ pounds Savoy cabbage, cored and sliced into ribbons about ¼ inch wide*
- *1½ cups grated Fontina Val d'Aosta cheese (about ⅓ pound)*
- *6 tablespoons freshly grated Parmesan cheese*

To make pappardelle, combine unbleached flour, buckwheat flour and salt in a bowl. Stir to blend. Turn out onto work surface. Beat eggs and oil together in same bowl. To assemble, knead, and stretch the dough, follow the directions for making fresh pasta on pages 23–25. When you have rolled the sheets to #5 setting, cut them by hand into noodles about 3 inches long and ½ inch wide. (These proportions yield slightly more than 1 pound pasta; save any extra and enjoy it boiled and buttered the next day.)

To make sauce, melt butter with olive oil in a 12-inch skillet over moderately low heat. Add sage leaves and fry slowly, turning occasionally, until they are crisp, 7 to 8 minutes. Lower heat if necessary to prevent burning. Transfer with tongs to paper towels to drain.

Add leeks to skillet and sauté until softened, about 5 minutes. Season highly with salt and pepper. Keep warm.

Bring a large pot of salted water—at least 5 quarts—to a boil. Add cabbage and boil until just tender, 3 to 5 minutes. Measure out a pound of pasta, add it to the pot with the cabbage, and cook until al dente. Drain, reserving about ½ cup of the cooking water. Transfer pasta and cabbage to a large warm bowl. Add leeks and toss to coat. Add Fontina and 4 tablespoons of the Parmesan and toss until cheese has melted, adding a little of the reserved cooking water if necessary to make a creamy sauce. Serve immediately on warm dishes, topping each serving with some fried sage leaves and a little additional Parmesan. Serves 6.

CAULIFLOWER

WHEN IT IS YOUNG AND MILD, CAULIFLOWER IS A FINE POINT OF DEPARTURE FOR A PASTA SAUCE. CHOP IT AND SIMMER IN TOMATO SAUCE WITH GREEN OLIVES OR IN TOMATO SAUCE WITH SAUSAGE AND FENNEL; TOSS WITH BÉCHAMEL, PROSCIUTTO AND NOODLES; OR BAKE IT WITH THE EAR-SHAPED ORECCHIETTE AND A GOOD DEAL OF CHEESE. IT IS AN ACCOMMODATING VEGETABLE, ONE THAT ADAPTS TO MANY SEASONINGS AND PREPARATIONS. ◢ THESE DAYS, MANY SUPERMARKETS SELL A PRETTY, PALE GREEN CAULIFLOWER CALLED BROCCOFLOWER. YOU CAN USE IT IN PLACE OF WHITE CAULIFLOWER AS IT TASTES MUCH THE SAME. FOR EITHER COLOR, LOOK FOR CAULIFLOWER THAT IS FIRM AND RELATIVELY UNBLEMISHED, AND WITH A COMPACT—NOT SPREADING—SURFACE. IT IS AVAILABLE IN GOOD QUALITY AND QUANTITY YEAR-ROUND. ◢ CAULIFLOWER LEAVES ARE PERFECTLY EDIBLE. ALTHOUGH I SUGGEST REMOVING THEM FOR THESE SAUCES, YOU CAN COOK THEM, CHOP THEM UP, AND ADD THEM TO YOUR SAUCE IF YOU PREFER.

PERCIATELLI WITH CAULIFLOWER, TOMATO, SAUSAGE AND PINE NUTS

IT'S SURPRISING HOW LITTLE SAUSAGE IT TAKES TO ADD RICHNESS AND COMPLEXITY TO THIS CAULIFLOWER SAUCE. A PINCH OF FENNEL SEED ALSO ADDS A PLEASING, LICORICE-LIKE FLAVOR. PERCIATELLI (ALSO KNOWN AS BUCATINI) LOOK LIKE THICK SPAGHETTI, BUT LOOK CLOSER: THEY HAVE A HOLE DOWN THE MIDDLE.

· *1 small head cauliflower (about 1 pound)*

· *⅓ cup pine nuts*

· *4 tablespoons olive oil*

· *4 ounces sweet or hot Italian sausage, removed from casing if necessary*

· *2 large cloves garlic, minced*

· *1½ cups strained canned tomatoes (pages 21–22)* →

◢ Preheat oven to 325°F. Bring a large pot of salted water—at least 5 quarts—to a boil over high heat. Meanwhile, remove cauliflower leaves and trim the base, leaving enough of it to hold the head together. Add to water and boil until tender but not mushy, about 8 minutes. Remove with tongs and let cool, then chop medium-fine. Reserve cooking water.

◢ Spread pine nuts on a baking sheet or pie pan and bake until lightly browned, 10 to 15 minutes, shaking pan occasionally so nuts brown evenly. Set aside.

◢ Put 1 tablespoon of the olive oil and the sausage meat in a 12-inch skillet. Cook over moderately low heat, stirring to break up sausage, until meat just loses its pink color, 3 to 4 minutes. Transfer contents of skillet to a small bowl. →

- ½ teaspoon fennel seed, crushed in a mortar or spice grinder
- ¼ teaspoon hot red pepper flakes (or less if using hot sausage)
- Salt
- Pinch sugar, optional
- 3 tablespoons minced parsley
- 1 pound dried perciatelli, bucatini or spaghetti
- 1 cup freshly grated pecorino romano cheese

Heat remaining 3 tablespoons oil in same skillet over moderately low heat. Add garlic and sauté 1 minute to release its fragrance. Add tomatoes, fennel seed, hot red pepper flakes, salt and sugar if tomatoes seem a bit tart. Bring to a simmer, adjust heat to maintain a simmer and cook 10 minutes, adding a few tablespoons of water when sauce gets too thick.

Stir in chopped cauliflower and simmer 5 minutes, adding a little water as necessary to thin the sauce. Stir in sausage, pine nuts and 2 tablespoons parsley. Taste and adjust seasoning. Keep warm.

Boil pasta until al dente in the same water you used to cook the cauliflower. Transfer pasta with tongs to a large warm bowl, allowing some water to cling to the pasta. Add sauce and toss. Add cheese and toss again, adding some of the hot pasta water as needed to help the sauce coat the noodles nicely. Serve immediately on warm dishes, topping each serving with a little of the remaining 1 tablespoon parsley. Serves 4.

ORECCHIETTE WITH CAULIFLOWER

I LOVE THE TASTE OF PUNGENT SHEEP'S MILK CHEESE WITH CAULIFLOWER. THIS PASTA DISH CALLS FOR TWO KINDS: A PECORINO ROMANO FOR GRATING FINE, AND A YOUNG PECORINO THAT WILL GRATE INTO COARSE SHREDS AND MELT NICELY. FOR THE LATTER, ASK YOUR CHEESE MERCHANT FOR TOSCANELLO (A YOUNG PECORINO), MANCHEGO (A SPANISH SHEEP'S MILK CHEESE) OR SOMETHING SIMILAR.

THIS DISH IS AT ITS MOST SUBLIME WHEN IT'S FINISHED UNDER A BROILER. IF YOU DON'T HAVE A BROILER, OR IF YOUR BROILER CAN'T ACCOMMODATE YOUR SKILLET, BAKE IN A PREHEATED 425°F OVEN UNTIL THE CHEESE HAS MELTED.

- 2 small cauliflowers (about 1¼ pounds each)
- ¼ cup olive oil
- 1 large yellow onion, minced
- 2 large cloves garlic, minced
- ¼ teaspoon hot red pepper flakes
- Salt
- 1 cup chicken or vegetable stock
- 4 tablespoons minced parsley
- 1 pound dried orecchiette ("little ears")
- ½ cup freshly grated pecorino romano cheese
- 2 cups freshly grated young pecorino cheese (see introduction)

Remove cauliflower leaves. Cut florets away from the thick core. Separate large florets with a knife into very small florets. You should have about 1½ pounds florets.

Preheat broiler.

Heat olive oil in a 12-inch skillet over moderately low heat. Add onion and sauté until soft and starting to color, about 15 minutes. Add garlic and sauté 1 minute to release its fragrance. Add hot red pepper flakes, cauliflower, salt to taste and stock. Bring to a simmer, then cover and adjust heat to maintain a simmer. Cook until cauliflower is tender but not mushy, 7 to 10 minutes. Uncover, if necessary, toward the end of the cooking to evaporate excess liquid; you want to have just 2 or 3 tablespoons of cooking juices remaining to moisten the pasta. Taste and adjust salt if necessary; the mixture should be highly seasoned. Stir in 3 tablespoons of the parsley.

Cook pasta in a large pot of boiling salted water until al dente. Drain and return to pasta pot. Add contents of skillet and toss well. Add pecorino romano and ½ cup of the young pecorino and toss again. Transfer to a large baking dish; I use an oval earthenware baking dish that measures about 15 by 10 by 3 inches. Sprinkle remaining 1½ cups young pecorino over the surface; broil until cheese has melted and is browned in spots. Top with remaining 1 tablespoon parsley. Serve on warm dishes. Serves 4.

PENNE WITH CAULIFLOWER SAUCE

THIS LOVELY RECIPE IS BORROWED FROM THE BACK OF THE DE CECCO PASTA BOX. I HAVE MODIFIED IT SLIGHTLY TO APPEAL TO MY TASTE AND TO FILL IN THE DETAILS THAT THE BOX COPY OMITS. I THINK IT'S PRETTIEST WHEN MADE WITH GREEN CAULIFLOWER; BROCCOLI WOULD ALSO WORK WELL.

· *1 medium cauliflower (about 1½ pounds)*

· *3 tablespoons unsalted butter*

· *1 tablespoon all-purpose flour*

· *1 cup milk, or as needed*

· *Salt and freshly ground black pepper*

· *2 ounces prosciutto di Parma, minced*

· *1 small yellow onion, minced*

· *½ cup chicken or beef stock*

· *1 pound penne rigate (ridged tubes) or gnocchetti rigati (large ridged tubes)*

· *½ cup freshly grated Parmesan cheese*

Bring a large pot of salted water — at least 5 quarts — to a boil. Meanwhile, remove cauliflower leaves and trim the base, leaving enough of it to hold the head together. Add cauliflower to pot and boil until tender, 10 to 15 minutes. Transfer to a colander with tongs and place under cold running water until it is cool. Drain well, then remove florets from the thick core and chop them medium-fine. If the core is tender and not woody, chop that as well; otherwise discard it. Reserve cooking water.

To make a bechamel sauce, melt 1 tablespoon of the butter in a small skillet over moderately low heat. Add flour and whisk to blend. Cook, whisking constantly, for a minute or two, then add 1 cup milk. Bring to a simmer, whisking often; then reduce heat to lowest setting and cook, whisking occasionally, until sauce no longer has a floury taste, about 20 minutes. Season with salt and pepper. Stir in prosciutto. Keep warm, thinning if necessary with a little additional milk or some stock. The béchamel should be on the thin side but not soupy. Keep warm.

Melt remaining 2 tablespoons butter in a 12-inch skillet over moderately low heat. Add onion and sauté until quite soft and sweet and lightly colored, about 15 minutes. Add chopped cauliflower, season with salt and pepper and stir to blend. Add stock and simmer until stock is almost fully absorbed. Keep warm.

Boil pasta until al dente in the same water you used to cook the cauliflower. Drain, reserving about ½ cup of the cooking water. Transfer pasta to a large warm bowl. Add contents of skillet and béchamel and toss to coat. Add cheese and toss again, adding a little of the reserved cooking water if needed to thin the sauce. (You may not need any if your béchamel is thin enough.) Serve immediately on warm dishes. Serves 4.

LINGUINE WITH CAULIFLOWER, TOMATO AND OLIVES

SWEET CAULIFLOWER, PEPPERY TOMATO SAUCE, FRUITY GREEN OLIVES, TANGY CHEESE. THESE FLAVORS ARE WONDERFUL TOGETHER. I PARTICULARLY LIKE IMPORTED BRINE-CURED PICHOLINE OLIVES IN THIS DISH, BUT USE WHICHEVER GREEN OLIVES YOU PREFER.

- ¼ cup olive oil
- 1 small yellow onion, minced
- 2 large cloves garlic, minced
- ¼ teaspoon hot red pepper flakes, or to taste
- 1½ cups strained canned tomatoes (pages 21–22)
- 2 tablespoons finely minced, oil-packed sun-dried tomato
- 1 medium cauliflower (about 1½ pounds)
- Salt
- 32 green olives, pitted and chopped
- 3 tablespoons minced parsley
- 1 pound dried linguine or spaghetti
- ¾ cup freshly grated pecorino romano cheese

Heat olive oil in a 12-inch skillet over moderately low heat. Add onion and sauté until soft and starting to color, about 15 minutes. Add garlic and sauté 1 minute to release its fragrance. Add hot red pepper flakes and strained tomatoes. Raise heat to moderate and simmer, stirring with a wooden spoon, until mixture has the texture of tomato sauce, 5 to 10 minutes. Stir in sun-dried tomato.

Meanwhile, bring a large pot of salted water—at least 5 quarts—to a boil. Remove cauliflower leaves and trim the base, leaving enough of it to hold the head together. Add cauliflower to water and boil until tender, 10 to 15 minutes. Remove with tongs and let cool, then chop into very small pieces. Reserve cooking water.

Add cauliflower to skillet, season with salt and stir to coat with sauce. Cover, bring to a simmer, then adjust heat to maintain a simmer and cook about 10 minutes to allow cauliflower to absorb the seasonings. Uncover and stir occasionally to make sure cauliflower is not sticking, adding hot water from the pot if needed. At the end, the cauliflower should be soft enough to collapse when pressed gently with a wooden spoon. When done, stir in olives and 2 tablespoons of the parsley. Taste and adjust seasoning. Sauce should be peppery.

Boil pasta until al dente in the same water you used to cook the cauliflower. Transfer with tongs to a large warm bowl. Add sauce and pecorino and toss to coat. Add hot pasta water as needed to thin the sauce. Serve immediately on warm dishes, garnishing each serving with a little of the remaining 1 tablespoon parsley. Serves 4.

CHARD
CHOOSE CHARD WITH CRISP, UNBLEMISHED LEAVES AND RELATIVELY NARROW RIBS. IT IS ONE OF THE FEW LEAFY GREENS THAT TOLERATES HOT WEATHER, SO YOU CAN USUALLY FIND IT IN GOOD SHAPE THROUGHOUT THE YEAR. MANY MARKETS CARRY BOTH GREEN AND RED SWISS CHARD, BUT I USE ONLY GREEN WITH PASTA; RED CHARD "BLEEDS" WHEN COOKED, STAINING THE PASTA RED. ✦ WITH ITS PRONOUNCED TASTE, CHARD CAN HANDLE STRONG FLAVORS SUCH AS ANCHOVY, HOT RED PEPPER FLAKES, FENNEL SEED, PANCETTA, PECORINO CHEESE OR SPICY TOMATO SAUCE. YOU WILL FIND ALL THESE INGREDIENTS PAIRED WITH CHARD IN THE FOLLOWING RECIPES. BECAUSE THE STEMS TAKE LONGER TO COOK THAN THE LEAVES DO, THE TWO ARE TYPICALLY SEPARATED BEFORE COOKING. YOU CAN MAKE A SAUCE WITH JUST THE STEMS, JUST THE LEAVES, OR BOTH.

SPAGHETTI WITH CHARD, ONIONS AND ANCHOVY BUTTER

THIS RECIPE USES ONLY THE CHARD LEAVES. SAVE THE WHITE RIBS AND SERVE THEM THE NEXT DAY SIMMERED IN TOMATO SAUCE OR BOILED, BUTTERED AND SPRINKLED WITH PARMESAN. OR MAKE SPAGHETTI WITH CHARD RIBS AND PANCETTA (PAGE 72).

- 24 whole black peppercorns
- 2 cloves garlic
- Salt
- 8 anchovy fillets
- 2 tablespoons unsalted butter, softened
- 2½ to 3 pounds green chard
- 3 tablespoons olive oil
- 2 medium yellow onions, thinly sliced
- 1 pound dried spaghetti

✦ To make anchovy butter, in a mortar, grind peppercorns, garlic and a pinch of salt to a paste. Add anchovies and grind until smooth. Add butter and blend until smooth. Set aside at room temperature so that it is soft when you are ready to sauce the pasta.

✦ Cut along edge of chard ribs to separate ribs from leaves. Save ribs for soup or for another pasta dish, if desired. Wash leaves in a sink filled with cold water. Drain in a colander but do not dry. Weigh out 1½ pounds of leaves, reserving the rest for another dish. Stack leaves, a few at a time, and cut crosswise into 1-inch-wide ribbons.

✦ Preheat oven to lowest setting. Heat 2 tablespoons of the olive oil in a 12-inch skillet over moderate heat. Add onions, season with salt, and sauté until soft, sweet and lightly colored, 15 to 20 minutes. Transfer onions to a bowl or plate and keep warm in oven. Add chard ribbons to same skillet along with a generous pinch of salt. (It will be bulky but will quickly cook down.) Cover and cook in just the water clinging to the leaves until chard is wilted and softened, 5 to 7 minutes, uncovering once or twice to stir. Keep warm. →

Cook pasta in a large pot of boiling salted water until al dente. If necessary, reheat chard just before pasta is ready. Remove chard from heat and stir in anchovy butter. Transfer pasta with tongs to a large warm bowl, leaving a little water clinging to the noodles. Add remaining 1 tablespoon oil and toss to coat. Add chard and onions and toss again. Serve immediately on warm dishes. Serves 4.

SPAGHETTI WITH CHARD RIBS AND PANCETTA

THIS RECIPE PAYS A DIVIDEND: YOU USE THE CHARD RIBS IN THE SAUCE AND COOK THE LEAVES FOR SALAD. TO MAKE THE SALAD, COOK LEAVES IN BOILING SALTED WATER UNTIL TENDER, 3 TO 4 MINUTES. DRAIN, OR LIFT THE LEAVES OUT WITH A SKIMMER AND SAVE THE WATER FOR COOKING PASTA. PLACE THE LEAVES IN A SIEVE UNDER COLD RUNNING WATER TO STOP THE COOKING. SQUEEZE BETWEEN YOUR HANDS TO REMOVE EXCESS MOISTURE. CHOP COARSELY, THEN DRESS THEM WITH OLIVE OIL, LEMON JUICE, MINCED GARLIC AND SALT.

· 4 pounds green chard

· 4 tablespoons olive oil

· 4 ounces pancetta, minced

· 2 large cloves garlic, minced

· Pinch hot red pepper flakes

· ¼ cup minced parsley

· Salt

· 1 pound dried spaghetti

· 1 cup freshly grated Parmesan cheese

Bring a large pot of salted water—at least 5 quarts—to a boil. Cut along edge of chard ribs to separate thick white ribs from leaves. Use leaves for a salad, if desired (see introduction). Add ribs to pot and boil until tender, about 5 minutes. Transfer to a sieve with tongs and shake dry, then pat dry with paper towels. Dice neatly into ⅓-inch squares. Reserve cooking water.

Heat 2 tablespoons of the olive oil in a 12-inch skillet over moderately low heat. Add pancetta and sauté until it begins to crisp, 3 to 5 minutes. Add garlic and hot red pepper flakes and sauté 1 minute to release garlic fragrance. Stir in chard stems and parsley and season highly with salt. Keep warm.

Boil pasta until al dente in the same water you used to cook the ribs. Transfer with tongs to a large warm bowl, allowing some water to cling to the noodles. Add remaining 2 tablespoons olive oil and ½ cup of the cheese. Toss to coat. Add chard mixture and remaining cheese and toss again, adding a little of the reserved cooking water as needed to moisten the noodles nicely. Serve immediately on warm dishes. Serves 4.

GEMELLI WITH TOMATO SAUCE, CHICK-PEAS AND CHARD

BEANS, GREENS AND TOMATOES ARE A HOLY TRINITY IN ITALIAN SOUPS AND STEWS AND EQUALLY COMPATIBLE IN SAUCES. IF YOU ADJUST PARBOILING TIME ACCORDINGLY, YOU CAN SUBSTITUTE FRESH SPINACH OR KALE FOR THE CHARD. (SPINACH WILTS IN SECONDS.) YOU CAN ALSO SUBSTITUTE WHITE BEANS FOR THE CHICK-PEAS, IF YOU PREFER. BUT DON'T OMIT THE FENNEL SEED! IT'S THE INGREDIENT THAT KNITS EVERYTHING TOGETHER.

· *2 medium bunches green chard (14 to 16 ounces each)*

· *¼ cup olive oil*

· *4 large cloves garlic, minced*

· *2 cups strained canned tomatoes (pages 21–22)*

· *½ teaspoon fennel seed, crushed in a mortar or spice grinder*

· *¼ teaspoon hot red pepper flakes*

· *Salt*

· *Pinch sugar, optional*

· *1 cup drained cooked chick-peas (rinsed and drained, if canned)*

· *1 pound dried gemelli ("twins") or gnocchetti rigati (large ridged tubes)*

· *¾ cup freshly grated pecorino romano cheese*

Bring a large pot of salted water—at least 5 quarts—to a boil. Cut along edge of chard ribs to separate thick white ribs from leaves. Wash leaves in a sink filled with cold water. Drain well in a colander. Weigh out ¾ pound. (The ribs and any remaining leaves can be boiled, drained and dressed with olive oil and lemon juice for a salad, as described on page 72. Or reserve the ribs for Spaghetti with Chard Ribs and Pancetta, page 72.) Add leaves to pot and boil until they wilt and soften slightly, about 3 minutes. Remove with a skimmer to a sieve and run under cold water to stop the cooking. When cool enough to handle, squeeze dry and chop coarsely. Set aside. Reserve cooking water.

Heat olive oil in a 12-inch skillet over moderately low heat. Add garlic and sauté 1 minute to release its fragrance. Add tomatoes, fennel seed, hot red pepper flakes and salt to taste. Bring to a simmer and taste. Add sugar if mixture seems too tart. Simmer 5 minutes, then add chick-peas and continue simmering until mixture is thick and saucelike, about 5 more minutes. Stir in chopped chard. Keep warm.

Boil pasta until al dente in the same water you used to cook the chard. Drain, reserving about ½ cup of the cooking water. Transfer pasta to a large warm bowl. Add contents of skillet and toss to coat. Add cheese and toss again, adding a little reserved cooking water as needed to help the sauce coat the noodles nicely. Serve immediately on warm dishes. Serves 4.

EGGPLANTS

EGGPLANTS

EGGPLANT AND PASTA ARE AS COMPANIONABLE AS BREAD AND BUTTER. THE FOLLOWING RECIPES OFFER THREE EXAMPLES OF THEIR SUCCESSFUL MARRIAGE, EACH ONE INCLUDING TOMATO OR TOMATO SAUCE, BUT EACH ONE DIFFERENT. ∅ YOU WILL FIND THE BEST-QUALITY EGGPLANTS IN THE MARKETS IN LATE SUMMER. WHETHER YOU ARE BUYING LARGE GLOBE EGGPLANTS OR THE SLENDER ASIAN OR ITALIAN TYPES, THE SIGNS OF QUALITY ARE THE SAME: THE EGGPLANT SHOULD FEEL FIRM AND SMOOTH, NOT SPONGY; IT SHOULD HAVE NO SOFT SPOTS OR BLEMISHES; AND IT SHOULD FEEL HEAVY FOR ITS SIZE. EGGPLANT DOESN'T LIKE TO BE REFRIGERATED; IF YOU CAN'T USE IT THE DAY YOU BUY IT, STORE IT IN A COOL PLACE IN A PLASTIC BAG.

FUSILLI WITH ROASTED EGGPLANT SAUCE

THERE MUST BE TWO DOZEN DIFFERENT WAYS TO COMBINE EGGPLANT AND TOMATO FOR PASTA SAUCE. HERE'S ONE OF MY FAVORITES—A NEAR-PURÉE OF ROASTED EGGPLANT SIMMERED IN RICH TOMATO SAUCE.

· 1½ pounds dark purple, slender Italian or Japanese eggplants

· 2 tablespoons extra virgin olive oil

· 1 cup Summer Tomato Sauce (page 140)

· Salt and freshly ground black pepper

· 3 tablespoons minced parsley

· 1 pound dried fusilli

· ⅔ cup freshly grated pecorino romano cheese

∅ Preheat oven to 450°F. Prick eggplants with a sharp knife in a couple of places, then place on a baking sheet or in a low-sided baking dish. Roast until tender when pierced, 45 to 50 minutes. When cool enough to handle, cut in half lengthwise, scrape the pulp away from the skin with a spoon and chop pulp until reduced to a near-purée. In a 12-inch skillet, combine chopped eggplant, olive oil, tomato sauce and salt and pepper to taste. Cook over moderately low heat, stirring often, for 10 minutes to blend the flavors. Stir in 2 tablespoons of the parsley.

∅ Cook pasta in a large pot of boiling salted water until al dente. Drain, reserving about ½ cup of the cooking water. Transfer pasta to a large warm bowl. Add sauce and toss to coat. Add all but ¼ cup cheese and toss again, adding a little of the reserved cooking water if needed to thin the sauce. Serve immediately on warm dishes, topping each portion with some of the remaining cheese and parsley. Serves 4.

PENNE WITH BROILED EGGPLANT AND TOMATO

SO MANY PASTA RECIPES FOR EGGPLANT CALL FOR PANFRYING IT IN LOTS OF OIL—HOT AND MESSY WORK. I SUSPECT THAT, LIKE ME, YOU'D RATHER BROIL THE EGGPLANT. IT ABSORBS LESS OIL, MAKES LESS MESS AND TASTES JUST AS GOOD; WHAT'S MORE, YOU CAN BROIL THE TOMATO ALONGSIDE TO MAKE YOUR SAUCE. IF YOU HAVE TWO OVENS, EACH WITH A BROILER, YOU CAN DOUBLE THE RECIPE EASILY. IT IS QUICKLY MADE, EASY AND DELICIOUS.

- *1 small globe eggplant (about ¾ pound)*
- *1 large ripe tomato (about ½ pound)*
- *3 tablespoons olive oil*
- *1 large clove garlic, minced*
- *Salt*
- *⅛ teaspoon hot red pepper flakes*
- *Approximately 1 teaspoon red or white wine vinegar*
- *½ pound dried penne rigate (ridged tubes) or gnocchetti rigati (large ridged tubes)*
- *2 tablespoons minced parsley*
- *12 fresh basil leaves, julienned*
- *½ cup freshly grated pecorino romano cheese*

Preheat broiler. Remove stem end of eggplant. Slice unpeeled eggplant into ¾-inch-thick rounds. Core tomato and cut in half horizontally. Arrange eggplant rounds and tomato halves on broiler pan. In a small bowl, stir together olive oil and garlic. Brush surface of eggplant and tomatoes with some of the oil. Season generously with salt. Position broiler pan 4 to 6 inches from the heat and broil until eggplant is lightly browned, about 5 minutes, brushing eggplant again with oil halfway through. Turn eggplant rounds and brush the other side with oil and season with salt. Continue broiling until second side is nicely browned and eggplant is cooked through but still firm enough to slice, about 5 minutes. Brush again with oil halfway through. By the time the eggplant is cooked, the tomato halves should be soft and sizzling.

With a serrated knife, cut eggplant rounds into ½-inch cubes. Transfer to a large warm bowl. Chop the soft tomatoes into a near-purée and add to bowl along with any accumulated juices. Add hot red pepper flakes and sprinkle the mixture with 1 teaspoon wine vinegar. Add any remaining garlic and oil. Toss mixture gently; taste and adjust seasoning with vinegar and salt. Keep warm in a low oven or at room temperature.

Cook pasta in a large pot of boiling salted water until al dente. Drain. Transfer to warm bowl containing eggplant mixture. Add parsley and basil. Toss to coat. Add ¼ cup of the cheese and toss again. Serve on warm dishes, topping each portion with some of the remaining ¼ cup cheese. Serves 2.

RIGATONI WITH FRIED EGGPLANT, TOMATO AND OLIVES

ASK A GOOD CHEESE MERCHANT FOR RICOTTA SALATA, AN ITALIAN SHEEP'S MILK CHEESE
AGED UNTIL IT IS FIRM ENOUGH TO GRATE. ITS PUNGENT FLAVOR IS PERFECT FOR RICH
TOMATO SAUCES LIKE THIS ONE.

- *1 pound dark purple, slender Italian or Japanese eggplants*
- *Salt*
- *5 tablespoons olive oil*
- *⅔ cup diced celery*
- *⅔ cup diced yellow onion*
- *4 cloves garlic, minced*
- *1½ pounds ripe plum tomatoes, peeled and seeded (page 22), then chopped*
- *Scant ¼ teaspoon hot red pepper flakes*
- *1 pound dried rigatoni*
- *Approximately 30 brine-cured green olives, preferably picholine, pitted and coarsely chopped*
- *¾ cup freshly grated ricotta salata or pecorino romano cheese*
- *2 tablespoons minced parsley*

✑ Remove stem ends of eggplants. Cut eggplants in half lengthwise, then cut eggplant into neat ½-inch cubes. Sprinkle with 1½ teaspoons salt and put the cubes in a sieve set over a bowl to drain for 1 hour. Stir them with your hands once or twice during that time. Pat dry with paper towels (no need to rinse).

✑ Heat 3 tablespoons of the olive oil in a 12- to 14-inch skillet over moderately high heat. Add eggplant cubes and sauté until they are nicely browned on all sides, about 10 minutes. (You can do this in two batches in a smaller skillet if necessary.) Transfer with a slotted spoon to several thicknesses of paper towels to drain.

✑ Reduce heat to moderately low. Add the remaining 2 tablespoons oil to skillet along with celery and onion. Sauté until softened, about 10 minutes. Add garlic and sauté 1 minute to release its fragrance. Add tomatoes and hot red pepper flakes. Raise heat to moderately high and cook, stirring often, until tomatoes have collapsed and formed a thick sauce, 15 or 20 minutes. Add water as necessary to keep sauce from sticking and to bring it to the desired consistency. Season to taste with salt.

✑ Cook pasta in a large pot of boiling salted water until al dente. Just before pasta is ready, stir eggplant and olives into tomato sauce and reheat gently over low heat. Drain pasta, reserving about ½ cup of the cooking water. Transfer pasta to a large warm bowl. Add contents of skillet and toss to coat, adding a little of the reserved cooking water if needed to help the sauce coat the pasta nicely. Serve immediately on warm dishes, topping each portion with cheese and parsley. Serves 4.

FENNEL

FENNEL

· Penne with Fennel, Tomato
and Olives

· Linguine with Braised Fennel, Walnuts,
Saffron and Cream

FENNEL

FENNEL BULB FENNEL WITH ITS LICORICE-LIKE FLAVOR APPEALS TO ME GREATLY IN PASTA SAUCE, ALTHOUGH IT IS RARELY USED THAT WAY IN ITALY. I LIKE IT BRAISED IN A SPICY TOMATO SAUCE OR CHOPPED AND SIMMERED IN A CREAM SAUCE WITH SAFFRON AND WALNUTS. ∅ LOOK FOR BULBS THAT ARE RELATIVELY UNBLEMISHED AND ON THE SMALL SIDE. IF THE OUTER LAYER IS THICK AND FIBROUS, PEEL IT BACK AND DISCARD IT. SOME MARKETS SELL BULB FENNEL (ALSO KNOWN AS ANISE OR FINOCCHIO) WITH THE STALKS AND FEATHERY LEAVES STILL ATTACHED. THE LEAVES CAN BE CHOPPED AND ADDED TO SALADS OR FISH DISHES; THE STALKS SHOULD BE DISCARDED. ∅ FENNEL IS A COOL-WEATHER VEGETABLE, MOST READILY AVAILABLE IN LATE FALL, WINTER AND SPRING.

2/8/99 — fennel flavor lost

PENNE WITH FENNEL, TOMATO AND OLIVES

· *1½ pounds fennel bulbs without stalks*

· *¼ cup olive oil*

· *3 large cloves garlic, minced*

· *¼ teaspoon hot red pepper flakes*

· *2 cups strained canned tomatoes (pages 21–22)*

· *1 tablespoon minced fresh oregano*

· *Pinch sugar, optional*

· *⅔ cup chopped black olives, preferably dry-cured or Niçoise*

· *1 pound dried penne rigate (ridged tubes)*

· *4 tablespoons minced parsley*

· *¾ cup freshly grated pecorino romano cheese*

IF YOU BUY FENNEL WITH THE STALKS ATTACHED, DON'T DISCARD THE FEATHERY LEAVES; CHOP THEM AND ADD TO GREEN SALAD, TOMATO SALAD, GREEN BEANS OR FISH DISHES. MAKE SURE YOU BUY ENOUGH FENNEL TO YIELD ABOUT 1½ POUNDS OF BULB AFTER TRIMMING OFF TOPS.

∅ Bring a large pot of salted water—at least 5 quarts—to a boil. Quarter the fennel bulbs lengthwise. If the outer layer looks thick and tough, remove it. Add the quartered bulbs to the pot and boil until tender, about 10 minutes. Remove with tongs to a sieve to drain. When cool enough to handle, core the quarters, then chop the flesh into small neat dice. You should have 1 to 1¼ pounds. Reserve cooking water.

∅ Heat olive oil in a 12-inch skillet over moderately low heat. Add garlic and sauté 1 minute to release its fragrance. Add hot red pepper flakes, tomatoes and oregano. Bring to a simmer. Taste and add sugar if mixture seems too tart. Simmer, stirring often, until sauce is thick and tasty, about 20 minutes. Stir in chopped fennel and olives. Keep warm, adding a little water as necessary to keep the sauce the proper consistency. Taste and adjust seasoning.

∅ Boil pasta until al dente in the same water you used to cook the fennel. Drain, reserving about ½ cup of the cooking water. Transfer pasta to a large warm bowl. Add sauce and toss. Add 3 tablespoons of the parsley and the cheese and toss again, adding as much of the cooking water as needed to help the sauce coat the noodles nicely. Serve immediately on warm dishes, topping each serving with a little of the remaining 1 tablespoon parsley. Serves 4.

LINGUINE WITH BRAISED FENNEL, WALNUTS, SAFFRON AND CREAM

FOR THIS RECIPE, YOU WILL NEED ABOUT 1 POUND OF TRIMMED, CORED AND CHOPPED FENNEL BULB. THREE MEDIUM FENNEL BULBS SHOULD YIELD WHAT YOU NEED. YOU CAN ALWAYS SLICE ANY LEFTOVER FENNEL PAPER-THIN AND ADD IT TO A GREEN SALAD. NOTE THAT YOU DON'T WANT TO ADD THE WALNUTS UNTIL YOU ARE READY TO TOSS THE SAUCE WITH THE PASTA. IF YOU HEAT THEM IN THE SAUCE, THEY WILL DISCOLOR IT SLIGHTLY.

· ½ cup walnuts

· 3 medium fennel bulbs, preferably with stalks and feathery leaves attached

· 2 tablespoons unsalted butter

· 2 tablespoons olive oil

· Salt and freshly ground black pepper

· 1 cup chicken stock

· ⅛ teaspoon loosely packed saffron threads (about 15 threads)

· ½ cup heavy cream

· 1 pound fresh linguine

· ¼ cup finely minced green onions (scallions), white and pale green parts only

· ¼ cup minced parsley

❧ Preheat oven to 350°F. Spread walnuts on a baking sheet or pie pan and toast until fragrant and lightly browned, about 15 minutes. Cool, then chop fine. Set aside.

❧ Cut off stalks from fennel bulbs, if attached. Coarsely chop enough of the leaves to measure 1 tablespoon; set aside.

❧ Quarter the bulbs lengthwise. If the outer layer looks thick and tough, remove it. Core the quarters. Chop the fennel into small neat dice. You should have about 1 pound total.

❧ Melt butter with oil in a 12-inch skillet over moderately low heat. Add diced fennel and season with salt and pepper. Toss to coat with seasonings. Add stock and saffron, bring to a simmer and cover. Adjust heat to maintain a brisk simmer and cook until fennel is tender and much of the liquid has evaporated, about 10 minutes. Stir in cream. Bring to simmer and cook briefly to incorporate the cream. Take care not to reduce it too much; fresh pasta absorbs a lot of sauce. Taste and adjust seasoning. Keep warm over low heat.

❧ Cook pasta in a large pot of boiling salted water until al dente. Drain, reserving about ½ cup of the cooking water. Transfer pasta to a large warm bowl. Add contents of skillet, walnuts, green onions and parsley. Toss to coat, adding a little of the reserved cooking water as needed to help the sauce coat the noodles nicely. Serve immediately on warm dishes, topping each serving with a few chopped fennel leaves, if available. Serves 4.

GARLIC / LEEKS / ONIONS
GREENS

GARLIC / LEEKS / ONIONS

- Penne with Leeks and Tomatoes
- Fettuccine with Leeks, Cream and Goat Cheese
- Linguine with Onion Sauce
- Spaghetti with Baked Garlic and Parsley

GREENS

- Spaghetti with Grilled Radicchio and Anchovy Butter
- Fettuccine with Endive, Radicchio and Gorgonzola
- Spaghettini with Escarole, Olives and Anchovies
- Fettuccine with Braised Endive, Red Peppers, Cream and Herbs
- Whole-Wheat Fettuccine with Winter Greens
- Fettuccine with Escarole, Pancetta and White Beans
- Whole-Wheat Spaghetti with Arugula

GARLIC / LEEKS / ONIONS
THESE AROMATIC VEGETABLES—USUALLY BEHIND THE SCENES IN SAUCES—CAN PLAY THE LEAD ROLE OCCASIONALLY. IT'S COMFORTING TO KNOW, WHEN THE CUPBOARD LOOKS BARE, THAT YOU CAN MAKE A SATISFYING SAUCE OUT OF LITTLE MORE THAN GARLIC AND OLIVE OIL, OR BUTTER AND ONIONS. ✑ ALTHOUGH GARLIC IS SOLD THE YEAR AROUND, IT DOES HAVE A SEASON. MOST OF THE DOMESTIC CROP IS HARVESTED IN SUMMER, AND THEN IT GOES INTO STORAGE. NEW-CROP GARLIC IS WONDERFULLY FIRM, WHITE AND MILD. IN STORAGE, IT GETS STRONGER AND SOMETIMES STARTS TO SPROUT. IF YOU CUT INTO A CLOVE AND FIND A GREENISH SPROUT IN THE CENTER, THAT GARLIC WILL ALMOST CERTAINLY TASTE STRONG. IT WILL HELP TO CUT AWAY THE SPROUTING CORE BEFORE CHOPPING THE CLOVE. ✑ A GARLIC BULB SHOULD FEEL FIRM AND HEAVY FOR ITS SIZE, AND ITS PAPERY OUTER SKIN SHOULD BE INTACT. ONCE THE SKIN IS BROKEN, THE CLOVES START TO DRY OUT. STORE IT IN A COOL, DARK, DRY PLACE, SUCH AS A LIDDED GARLIC CELLAR. ✑ LEEKS, A MEMBER OF THE ONION FAMILY, ARE USUALLY SOLD WITH A FAIR AMOUNT OF DARK LEAFY GREENS STILL ATTACHED. THE DARK GREEN LEAVES SHOULD BE CUT AWAY AND DISCARDED OR RESERVED FOR FLAVORING STOCK. THE PRIZED SECTION OF THE LEEK IS THE WHITE AND PALE GREEN PART. LARGE LEEKS CAN BE TOUGH AND HAVE A WOODY CORE; CHOOSE SMALL LEEKS WHEN POSSIBLE. WHATEVER THEIR SIZE, LEEKS TEND TO TRAP DIRT AND NEED TO BE WELL WASHED; HALVE THEM AND FLUSH BETWEEN THE LAYERS WITH WATER. FALL AND SPRING ARE PEAK TIMES FOR LEEKS, BUT THEY ARE USUALLY AVAILABLE THE YEAR AROUND. TO STORE, REFRIGERATE IN A PERFORATED PLASTIC BAG. ✑ I PREFER YELLOW ONIONS FOR MOST PASTA SAUCES. WHITE ONIONS HAVE A SHARPER TASTE, AND RED ONIONS LOSE THEIR COLOR WHEN COOKED, TURNING SLIGHTLY GRAY. I ALSO FREQUENTLY USE GREEN ONIONS (SCALLIONS) WHEN I WANT A FRESH BUT MILD ONION TASTE—WITH PEAS, FOR EXAMPLE. WHEN BUYING YELLOW ONIONS, LOOK FOR FIRM ONES WITH NO SIGNS OF SOOT OR MOLD. STORE THEM IN A COOL, DARK, DRY PLACE. GREEN ONIONS SHOULD HAVE FRESH-LOOKING, CRISP GREEN LEAVES THAT SHOW NO SIGNS OF WILTING OR DECAY. STORE THEM IN A PERFORATED PLASTIC BAG IN THE REFRIGERATOR CRISPER.

PENNE WITH LEEKS AND TOMATOES

COOKING THE LEEKS OVER A BRISK FLAME UNTIL THEY CARAMELIZE SLIGHTLY GIVES THIS SAUCE A GENTLE SWEETNESS. I WOULD PASS THE PARMESAN AT THE TABLE BECAUSE SOME PEOPLE MAY PREFER THIS DISH WITHOUT IT.

- *Approximately 1½ pounds leeks*
- *¼ cup olive oil*
- *Salt and freshly ground black pepper*
- *1 pound ripe plum tomatoes, peeled and seeded (page 22), then chopped*
- *1 cup chicken stock*
- *¼ cup heavy cream*
- *3 tablespoons minced parsley*
- *1 pound dried penne rigate (ridged tubes)*
- *Freshly grated Parmesan cheese for passing*

Cut off root ends and dark green leaves of leeks. You should have about 1 pound. Cut leeks in half lengthwise and wash well. Cut in half again lengthwise, then cut crosswise at ¾-inch intervals, discarding any core at the root end.

Heat olive oil in a 12-inch skillet over moderately high heat. Add leeks and season well with salt and pepper. Toss to coat with oil. Sauté briskly, stirring often, until leeks soften a little and brown lightly in spots, 6 to 8 minutes. Add tomatoes and continue to cook over brisk heat, stirring almost constantly with a wooden spoon, until tomatoes collapse and begin to form a sauce, 5 to 10 minutes. Mixture will be very thick. Add stock, reduce heat to moderately low and simmer, stirring, until stock is incorporated and reduced slightly, about 3 minutes. Stir in cream and 2 tablespoons of the parsley. Taste and adjust seasoning.

Cook pasta in a large pot of boiling salted water until al dente. Drain, reserving about ½ cup of the cooking water. Transfer pasta to a large warm bowl. Add sauce and toss to coat, adding enough of the reserved cooking water to help the sauce coat the noodles nicely. Serve immediately on warm dishes, topping each serving with some of the remaining 1 tablespoon parsley. Pass Parmesan at the table. Serves 4.

FETTUCCINE WITH LEEKS, CREAM AND GOAT CHEESE

THIS IS A RICHLY SATISFYING DISH, BEST SERVED IN SMALL PORTIONS. SHARE IT THREE WAYS AS A MAIN COURSE, WITH A SALAD FIRST; OR DIVIDE IT FOUR WAYS AS A FIRST COURSE.

- *Approximately 1¼ pounds leeks*
- *2 tablespoons unsalted butter*
- *Salt and freshly ground black pepper*
- *½ cup chicken stock*
- *½ cup heavy cream*
- *2 ounces mild goat cheese, such as French Montrachet or Bucheron, cut into small pieces while cold*
- *½ pound fresh egg or spinach fettuccine*
- *2 tablespoons minced parsley*

❦ Cut off root ends and dark green leaves of leeks. You should have about ¾ pound. Cut leeks in half lengthwise and wash well. Thinly slice crosswise, discarding any core at the root end.

❦ Melt butter in a 10-inch skillet over moderate heat. Add leeks and sauté, stirring, until they are coated with butter. Season well with salt and pepper. Cover, reduce heat to moderately low and cook 15 minutes, uncovering occasionally to stir and make sure leeks aren't sticking. After 15 minutes, they should be soft and just starting to brown in places. Uncover and add stock and cream. Bring to a simmer, then turn off heat and stir in half of the goat cheese. Taste and adjust seasoning; sauce should be peppery.

❦ Cook pasta in a large pot of boiling salted water until al dente. If sauce has cooled off, reheat it gently; you don't want to reduce it much or it will be too thick. Drain pasta, reserving ¼ cup of the cooking water. Transfer pasta to skillet along with 1 tablespoon of the parsley and toss. Add remaining goat cheese. Toss again. If sauce looks too thick, add some of the reserved cooking water and toss again. Serve immediately on warm dishes. Garnish each serving with some of the remaining 1 tablespoon parsley and a grind of black pepper. Serves 3 or 4.

LINGUINE WITH ONION SAUCE

COOKED SLOWLY, ONIONS MELT DOWN TO A GENTLE, SWEET, VELVETY SAUCE THAT BENEFITS FROM A FINAL SPLASH OF MELLOW BALSAMIC VINEGAR.

❧ Melt butter with olive oil and pancetta in a 14-inch skillet over moderately low heat. Cook, stirring occasionally, until pancetta just starts to crisp, 3 to 5 minutes. Add onions and stir to coat with fat. Season with salt and pepper. Cover and cook over moderate heat until onions are meltingly soft and very sweet, 35 to 45 minutes. Uncover occasionally and stir with a wooden spoon to prevent sticking. When done, stir in balsamic vinegar to taste; you want just a hint of tartness to balance the sweet onions. Keep warm.

❧ Cook pasta in a large pot of boiling salted water until al dente. Lift out with tongs, leaving a little water clinging to the noodles, and transfer to skillet. Toss to coat with sauce. Add a little more hot pasta water if needed to help the sauce coat the noodles nicely. Serve immediately on warm dishes. Garnish each serving with parsley. Serves 4.

· 2 tablespoons unsalted butter

· 2 tablespoons olive oil

· 3 ounces pancetta, minced

· 6 medium yellow onions
  (about 3 pounds), thinly sliced

· Salt and freshly ground
  black pepper

· 1½ to 2 tablespoons
  balsamic vinegar

· 1 pound dried linguine
  or spaghetti

· 2 tablespoons minced parsley

SPAGHETTI WITH BAKED GARLIC AND PARSLEY

FEW PASTA DISHES PROVIDE AS MUCH SIMPLE SATISFACTION AS SPAGHETTI WITH GARLIC. WHEN YOU THINK YOU HAVE NO ENERGY TO COOK AND NOTHING IN THE HOUSE TO COOK WITH, YOU CAN PROBABLY STILL MANAGE TO CHOP SOME GARLIC, HEAT IT IN OLIVE OIL WITH PEPPER FLAKES AND PARSLEY AND TOSS IT WITH HOT PASTA. HERE'S A VARIATION, MADE WITH A HEAP OF WHOLE CLOVES BAKED UNTIL SOFT AND MILD. PLEASE NOTE THAT STRONG GARLIC WILL ONLY GET STRONGER WHEN BAKED, SO SAVE THIS RECIPE FOR THOSE TIMES WHEN YOU HAVE FIRM WHITE GARLIC CLOVES WITH NO SIGNS OF SPROUTING.

✐ Preheat oven to 375°F. Put garlic cloves, rosemary sprig, hot red pepper flakes, olive oil and a generous pinch of salt in a ramekin small enough that the oil comes almost to the top of the cloves. Cover and bake until cloves are soft and very lightly colored, about 25 minutes. Do not allow them to color much or they will taste strong. Remove and discard rosemary sprig.

✐ Cook pasta in a large pot of boiling salted water until al dente. Transfer with tongs to a large warm bowl, allowing some water to cling to the noodles. Add contents of ramekin and the parsley and toss. Serve immediately on warm dishes. Serves 4.

· 48 garlic cloves (from about 2 bulbs), peeled and then halved if large

· One 3-inch fresh rosemary sprig

· ¼ teaspoon hot red pepper flakes

· 6 tablespoons extra virgin olive oil

· Salt

· 1 pound dried spaghetti

· ¼ cup minced parsley

GREENS

GREENS PASTA MAKES A WELCOME FOIL FOR PLEASANTLY PUNGENT GREENS: ARUGULA, COLLARDS, KALE, BELGIAN ENDIVE, ESCAROLE OR SPICY MIXED BABY GREENS. EVEN THE ASSERTIVELY BITTER RADICCHIO— MORE A "RED" THAN A "GREEN"—CAN BE TAMED FOR PASTA: I LIKE TO BLANCH IT, THEN GRILL IT AND TOSS IT WITH HOT PASTA AND ANCHOVY BUTTER (BELOW). ✑ MOST OF THESE GREENS ARE COOL-WEATHER CROPS, MORE ABUNDANT IN SPRING, WINTER AND FALL THAN IN SUMMER. GREENS TEND TO GET TOUGHER AND STRONGER TASTING AS THEY GROW. WITH ARUGULA, COLLARDS AND KALE, LOOK FOR YOUNG, TENDER LEAVES. BELGIAN ENDIVE SHOULD FEEL FIRM AND HAVE FEW OR NO BLEMISHES; SIMILARLY, ESCAROLE SHOULD BE FREE OF BLEMISHES AND CRISP. FOR RADICCHIO, CHOOSE HEADS THAT ARE HEAVY AND FIRM, WITH NO SIGNS OF BROWNING.

SPAGHETTI WITH GRILLED RADICCHIO AND ANCHOVY BUTTER

GRILLING RADICCHIO IMPARTS A SUBTLE SMOKY FLAVOR THAT IS ABSOLUTELY DELICIOUS. CHOP IT UP AND TOSS IT WITH HOT PASTA AND ANCHOVY BUTTER FOR A REAL TREAT. I LIKE TO BLANCH THE RADICCHIO BRIEFLY FIRST TO REMOVE A LITTLE BITTERNESS, BUT YOU MAY CHOOSE NOT TO. JUST GRILL IT A LITTLE MORE SLOWLY AND SLIGHTLY LONGER.

IT HELPS TO HAVE TWO COOKS FOR THIS DISH: ONE TO MIND THE PASTA AND ANOTHER TO MIND THE GRILL.

- *36 whole black peppercorns*
- *2 small cloves garlic*
- *Salt*
- *8 anchovy fillets*
- *3 tablespoons unsalted butter*
- *2 large or 4 small heads radicchio (1½ pounds total weight)*
- *2 tablespoons olive oil*
- *1 pound dried spaghetti*
- *2 tablespoons minced parsley*

✑ Prepare a medium-hot charcoal fire and preheat oven to lowest setting.

✑ To make anchovy butter, in a mortar, grind peppercorns, garlic and a generous pinch of salt to a paste. Add anchovies and grind until smooth. Add butter and blend until smooth. Set aside at room temperature so that it is soft when you are ready to sauce the pasta.

✑ Bring a large pot of salted water to a boil. Cut radicchio heads in half through cores. Add to pot and blanch 30 to 45 seconds (the shorter time for small heads). Drain, pressing gently to release excess moisture. Transfer to paper towels to absorb moisture. If using large heads, cut each half in half again through the core. Put olive oil on a plate with a large pinch of salt. Add radicchio quarters to plate and turn to coat with oil on all sides.

✑ Grill radicchio on all sides until lightly browned and almost tender throughout; it's nice to leave them still slightly crunchy in the center. →

The best method is to brown the radicchio lightly first by cooking it over direct heat, then move it away from direct heat to finish cooking. It will take 5 to 8 minutes. Keep grill covered as much as possible to give radicchio a smoky taste. When done, transfer radicchio to a plate and keep warm in a low oven.

❍ Cook pasta in a fresh pot of boiling salted water (the radicchio water will be bitter) until al dente. Just before the pasta is ready, thinly slice radicchio crosswise, discarding core. Put anchovy butter in a large warm bowl. Add radicchio and toss to coat with melting butter. Transfer pasta to bowl with tongs, leaving a little water clinging to the noodles. Add 1 tablespoon parsley and toss. Serve immediately on warm dishes. Top each serving with a little of the remaining 1 tablespoon parsley. Serves 4.

FETTUCCINE WITH ENDIVE, RADICCHIO AND GORGONZOLA

CHEESE AND BUTTER MELT IN THE HEAT OF THE HOT PASTA TO MAKE A SIMPLE "SAUCE." THE COMBINATION OF TANGY GORGONZOLA, TOASTED PINE NUTS AND SLIGHTLY BITTER BROILED GREENS IS A LOVELY ONE.

· ¼ cup pine nuts

· 3 tablespoons unsalted butter, at room temperature, in small pieces

· ⅓ pound Italian Gorgonzola cheese, at room temperature, in small pieces

· ¼ cup minced parsley

· ¾ pound Belgian endives, heads halved lengthwise

· ¾ pound radicchio, heads halved through the core or quartered if large

❍ Preheat oven to 325°F. Spread pine nuts on a baking sheet or pie pan and bake until lightly browned, 10 to 15 minutes, shaking pan occasionally so nuts brown evenly. Transfer pine nuts to a large serving bowl. Add butter, cheese and parsley. Set aside.

❍ Preheat broiler. Remove a thin slice from the rounded side of each endive and radicchio half so that they will stand up straight, then arrange halves cut side up on broiler pan. Brush with olive oil. Season with salt and pepper. Position broiler pan as far as possible from the heat source. Broil a few minutes until vegetables are nicely browned. Turn, brush with oil and broil until the second side is browned. (If necessary, transfer the broiler pan to a 350°F oven and continue to bake until vegetables are tender.)

❍ Preheat oven to lowest setting. Working quickly while vegetables are hot, core the endive halves and slice crosswise into ribbons ¼ inch wide. If radicchio is in halves, cut the halves in half again to make quarter wedges. Remove cores and slice

- Olive oil for brushing on vegetables
- Salt and freshly ground black pepper
- 1 pound fresh fettuccine

crosswise into ribbons ¼ inch wide. Add endive and radicchio to bowl holding butter and cheese. Keep warm in oven.

❦ Cook pasta in a large pot of boiling salted water until al dente. Drain, reserving about ½ cup of the cooking water. Transfer pasta to bowl with endive and

radicchio and toss until butter and cheese are melted, adding as much of the reserved cooking water as needed to make the noodles glisten. Serve immediately on warm dishes. Serves 4.

SPAGHETTINI WITH ESCAROLE, OLIVES AND ANCHOVIES

THIS 10-MINUTE PASTA SAUCE IS SURE TO PLEASE ANYONE WHO LIKES PUNGENT FLAVORS. AND AS ANYONE WHO MAKES IT WILL DISCOVER, THE SEASONED ESCAROLE ALONE—WITHOUT PASTA AND CHEESE—WOULD MAKE A WONDERFUL SIDE DISH.

- 2 medium heads escarole (about ¾ pound each)
- ¼ cup olive oil
- 4 large cloves garlic, minced
- 4 anchovy fillets, minced to a paste
- ¼ cup chopped pitted Niçoise olives
- ¼ teaspoon hot red pepper flakes, or to taste
- Salt
- 1 pound dried spaghettini
- ⅔ cup freshly grated pecorino romano cheese

❦ Bring a large pot of salted water—at least 5 quarts—to a boil. Add 1 whole escarole, stem end down. Simmer for 1½ minutes, then transfer with tongs to a sieve and place under cold running water to cool. When cool enough to handle, squeeze dry. Repeat with second head of escarole. (You can blanch both at once if your pot is big enough.) Halve heads through the cores and cut away cores. Cut each half crosswise into ½-inch-wide ribbons. Reserve cooking water.

❦ Heat olive oil in a 12-inch skillet over moderately low heat. Add garlic and sauté 1 minute to release its fragrance. Add anchovies and stir to blend. Add olives,

hot red pepper flakes and escarole. Toss to coat escarole with seasonings. Season to taste with salt. Keep warm over low heat.

❦ Boil pasta until al dente in the same water you used to cook the escarole. Transfer pasta with tongs to a large warm bowl, allowing a little water to cling to the noodles. Add contents of skillet and toss to blend. Add half of the cheese and toss again, adding a little of the hot pasta water if necessary to keep the noodles moist. Serve immediately on warm dishes, topping each portion with a little of the remaining cheese. Serves 4.

FETTUCCINE WITH BRAISED ENDIVE, RED PEPPERS, CREAM AND HERBS

A HANDFUL OF CHOPPED HERBS ADDED TO THE SAUCE AT THE LAST MINUTE GIVES THIS PASTA DISH A BURST OF FRESH FLAVOR.

· 2 tablespoons unsalted butter

· 2 tablespoons olive oil

· 1 pound Belgian endives, halved, cored and thinly sliced lengthwise

· Salt and freshly ground black pepper

· 2 red bell peppers, roasted, peeled, seeded, deribbed and very thinly sliced lengthwise (page 110)

· ½ cup heavy cream

· ¼ cup chicken stock

· 1 pound fresh fettuccine

· ¼ cup minced parsley

· ¼ cup minced fresh chives

· 2 tablespoons minced fresh mint

Melt butter with oil in a 12-inch skillet over moderate heat. Add endives, season with salt and pepper and toss to coat with fat. Cook, stirring or tossing occasionally, until endives are wilted but not completely soft, about 5 minutes. Add roasted peppers and toss again. Add cream and stock. Bring to a simmer and simmer until reduced to a saucelike consistency. Taste and adjust seasoning. Keep warm.

Cook pasta in a large pot of boiling salted water until al dente. Drain, reserving about ½ cup of the cooking water. Transfer pasta to a large warm bowl. Quickly stir parsley, chives and mint into sauce and then pour over pasta. Toss to coat, adding some of the reserved cooking water as needed to thin the sauce. Serve immediately on warm dishes. Serves 4.

WHOLE-WHEAT FETTUCCINE WITH WINTER GREENS

I SO ENJOY THE NUTTY FLAVOR OF FRESH WHOLE-WHEAT PASTA THAT I PREFER TO KEEP THE
SAUCE SIMPLE—JUST WILTED GREENS WITH FRUITY OLIVE OIL AND GARLIC. USE WHATEVER
DARK LEAFY GREENS LOOK BEST AND APPEAL TO YOU MOST. CONSIDER KALE, MUSTARD
GREENS, TURNIP GREENS, SPINACH, BROCCOLI RABE OR ARUGULA. THE COOKING TIME WILL
VARY SLIGHTLY FOR EACH GREEN, BUT THE METHOD IS THE SAME. FOR A VARIATION, REDUCE
THE AMOUNT OF TRIMMED GREENS TO 3/4 POUND AND ADD 1 CUP DRAINED COOKED CHICK-
PEAS (RINSED AND DRAINED, IF CANNED) TO THE SKILLET WITH THE GREENS.

For the whole-wheat fettuccine:

· *1 ½ cups whole-wheat flour*

· *1 ½ cups unbleached
all-purpose flour*

· *Large pinch salt*

· *4 eggs*

· *1 tablespoon olive oil*

For the sauce:

· *1 ¼ to 1 ⅓ pounds dark
leafy greens (see introduction)*

· *¼ cup extra virgin olive oil,
plus additional extra virgin
olive oil, for garnish*

· *4 cloves garlic, minced*

· *Salt and freshly ground
black pepper*

To make fettuccine, stir together flours and salt in a bowl. Turn out onto work surface. In the same bowl, whisk eggs and oil to blend. To assemble, knead and stretch the dough, and to cut the fettuccine, follow the directions for making fresh pasta on pages 23–25. (This recipe yields slightly more than 1 pound of noodles. Save any extra and enjoy them boiled and buttered the next day.)

To make sauce, cut away any tough ribs and stems from leaves. You should have about 1 pound trimmed greens.

Bring a large pot of salted water—at least 5 quarts—to a boil over high heat. Add greens and boil until just tender; plan on a few seconds for spinach to a few minutes for kale or broccoli rabe. Lift greens out with tongs or a skimmer and transfer to a sieve. Place under cold running water to stop the cooking.

Drain and squeeze dry, then chop coarsely. Reserve cooking water.

Heat ¼ cup olive oil in a 12-inch skillet over moderately low heat. Add garlic and sauté 1 minute to release its fragrance. Add chopped greens and season generously with salt and pepper. Toss to separate and coat with oil. Keep warm, adding a few tablespoons of water if necessary to keep greens moist and shiny.

Boil pasta until al dente in the same water you used to cook the greens. Drain, reserving about ½ cup of the cooking water. Transfer pasta to a large warm bowl. Add contents of skillet and toss, adding a little of the reserved water as needed to moisten the dish. Serve on warm dishes. Drizzle a generous teaspoon of olive oil over each serving. Serves 4.

FETTUCCINE WITH ESCAROLE, PANCETTA AND WHITE BEANS

ESCAROLE IS ONE OF THOSE SLIGHTLY BITTER WINTER GREENS THAT CAN STAND UP TO A LIT-
TLE COOKING. BLANCHING MODERATES ITS BITTER EDGE AND MAKES IT SOFT ENOUGH TO
TWIRL WITH FRESH LINGUINE. COMBINED WITH WELL-SEASONED WHITE BEANS AND PEPPERY
PANCETTA, IT MAKES A STURDY WINTER PASTA SAUCE.

· 4 tablespoons extra virgin
  olive oil

· 3 ounces pancetta, minced

· 4 large cloves garlic, minced

· 1 cup drained cooked
  cannellini beans or other
  white beans (rinsed and
  drained, if canned)

· Salt and freshly ground
  black pepper

· 1 pound escarole, preferably
  1 large head

· 1 pound fresh fettuccine

· Freshly grated pecorino
  romano cheese for passing

❡ Heat 2 tablespoons of the olive oil, the pancetta and garlic in a 12-inch skillet over moderately low heat until pancetta begins to crisp, 3 to 5 minutes. Add beans, season with salt and a good deal of black pepper and stir to coat with seasonings. Add ½ cup water and simmer for about 5 minutes to flavor the beans.

❡ Preheat oven to lowest setting. Bring a large pot of salted water — at least 5 quarts — to a boil. Plunge whole escarole, stem end down, into boiling water and blanch for 2 minutes. Remove with tongs to a sieve and place under cold running water to cool. When cool enough to handle, squeeze dry. Halve through core and cut away core. Cut each half crosswise into ⅓-inch-wide ribbons. Add escarole to skillet; stir to blend. Taste and adjust seasoning. Keep warm. Reserve cooking water.

❡ Put remaining 2 tablespoons olive oil in a large bowl and place in oven. Boil pasta in the same water you used to cook the escarole. Drain, reserving about ½ cup of the cooking water. Transfer pasta to the warmed bowl and toss to coat with oil. Add sauce and toss again, adding a little of the reserved water if needed to help the sauce coat the noodles nicely. Serve immediately on warm dishes. Pass the cheese separately. Serves 4.

WHOLE-WHEAT SPAGHETTI WITH ARUGULA

THIS IS ONE OF THOSE ASTONISHINGLY SIMPLE SAUCES THAT YOU CAN MAKE IN THE TIME IT TAKES TO COOK THE PASTA. IN MY NEIGHBORHOOD MARKETS, I CAN BUY YOUNG ARUGULA ALREADY WASHED AND DRIED—A REAL TIME-SAVER. IF YOUR MARKET DOESN'T SELL IT THAT WAY, YOU'LL NEED TO WASH IT CAREFULLY AND DRY IT THOROUGHLY IN A SALAD SPINNER OR IN TOWELS. LOOK FOR YOUNG ARUGULA WITH SMALL LEAVES. IF YOU'RE UNSURE OF ITS AGE, TASTE A LEAF. WHEN YOUNG, IT TASTES NUTTY AND MILD; OLDER ARUGULA CAN BE PEPPERY, EVEN HOT.

ARUGULA, LIKE MOST DEEP-GREEN LEAFY VEGETABLES, IS HIGH IN VITAMINS A AND C AND IRON. PAIRED WITH WHOLE-WHEAT SPAGHETTI, IT MAKES A SIMPLE DINNER THAT'S SIMULTANEOUSLY HEALTHFUL, DELICIOUS AND QUICK.

· 4 tablespoons extra virgin olive oil

· 12 cloves garlic, thinly sliced

· ¼ teaspoon hot red pepper flakes

· ¾ pound arugula leaves

· Salt

· 1 pound dried whole-wheat spaghetti

· ¾ cup freshly grated pecorino romano cheese

❦ Preheat oven to lowest setting. Heat 2 tablespoons of the olive oil in a 12-inch skillet over moderately low heat. Add garlic and hot red pepper flakes and cook until garlic is soft and mild, about 10 minutes. Add arugula (it will be bulky but will quickly cook down) and salt to taste. Toss with tongs until arugula has just barely wilted, about 2 minutes. Remove from heat. Put the remaining 2 tablespoons oil in a large bowl and set bowl in oven.

❦ Cook pasta in a large pot of boiling salted water until al dente. Just before it is done, reheat arugula gently. Transfer pasta with tongs to the warm bowl, leaving a little water clinging to the noodles. Toss well. Add contents of skillet and ½ cup of the cheese and toss again. Serve immediately on warm dishes. Top with remaining cheese. Serves 4.

MUSHROOMS

MUSHROOMS

I HAVE MADE ALL THE FOLLOWING MUSHROOM SAUCES WITH THE COMMON CULTIVATED *AGARICUS BISPORUS* MUSHROOMS FOUND IN SUPERMARKETS. IF YOU HAVE ACCESS TO WILD MUSHROOMS OR WANT TO PURCHASE THEM, YOU CAN SUBSTITUTE THEM, ALTHOUGH YOU MAY NEED TO MAKE SOME TIMING ADJUSTMENTS. I FIND THAT WILD MUSHROOMS USUALLY NEED TO COOK LONGER THAN CULTIVATED COMMON MUSHROOMS DO. ❂ BECAUSE SUPERMARKET MUSHROOMS DON'T HAVE A LOT OF CHARACTER, I PAIR THEM WITH OTHER INGREDIENTS THAT DO. IN THE FOLLOWING RECIPES, YOU'LL FIND THEM BRAISED WITH TOMATOES, PANCETTA AND ROSEMARY; BROWNED IN BUTTER AND TOSSED WITH FRIED SAGE LEAVES; PARTNERED WITH CHESTNUTS, THYME AND CREAM; AND SIMMERED WITH CREAM AND INTENSELY ARO-MATIC DRIED PORCINI. ❂ CULTIVATED MUSHROOMS ARE GROWN INDOORS IN A CONTROLLED ENVIRONMENT, SO THEY ARE AVAILABLE THE YEAR AROUND. LOOK FOR FIRM, NOT SPONGY, MUSHROOMS WITH SMOOTH, UNBLEMISHED CAPS. THE CAPS SHOULD BE TIGHTLY CLOSED UNDERNEATH, WITH NO GILLS SHOWING. MUSHROOMS DO NOT KEEP WELL; IF YOU CAN'T USE THEM THE DAY YOU BUY THEM, REFRIGERATE THEM IN A PAPER BAG.

FETTUCCINE WITH MUSHROOMS, CHESTNUTS AND CREAM

FRESH CHESTNUTS ARE AN AUTUMN TREAT, USUALLY SHOWING UP IN MY LOCAL MARKETS IN EARLY NOVEMBER AND DISAPPEARING IN A FEW WEEKS. PEELING THEM IS TEDIOUS—RECRUIT SOME HELPERS—BUT YOU WILL LOVE THE GENTLE SWEETNESS THEY ADD TO THIS PASTA SAUCE.

- ¾ *pound chestnuts*
- *2 tablespoons olive oil*
- ¾ *pound mushrooms, halved if large, then sliced*
- *Salt and freshly ground black pepper*
- *2 tablespoons unsalted butter*
- *1 small yellow onion, minced*
- *2 teaspoons minced fresh thyme*
- *1 cup chicken stock →*

❂ Cut an X in the flat side of each chest-nut. In a saucepan, boil chestnuts in water to cover for 10 minutes, then remove from heat. Remove them from the hot water one at a time with a slotted spoon and peel while hot, removing the tough outer shell and the paper-thin brown skin. Chop coarsely.

❂ Heat olive oil in a 12-inch skillet over high heat. Add mushrooms, season with salt and pepper, and sauté until they are nicely browned, 5 to 8 minutes. Transfer to a bowl.

❂ Let skillet cool for a minute or two, then add butter and melt over moderately low heat. Add onion and sauté until very soft, about 10 minutes. Add chopped chestnuts and thyme; season with salt and pepper. Add stock, bring to a simmer, then cover and adjust heat to maintain a simmer. Cook until chestnuts are tender, 12 to 15 minutes. Uncover and stir in →

· 1 cup heavy cream

· 2 tablespoons minced parsley

· 1 pound fresh fettuccine
or linguine

reserved mushrooms and the cream. Simmer briefly to reduce slightly; do not reduce too much as fresh pasta absorbs a lot of sauce. Taste and adjust seasoning. Stir in parsley and keep warm.

Cook pasta in a large pot of boiling salted water until al dente. Drain, reserving about 1 cup of the cooking water. Transfer pasta to a large warm bowl. Add sauce and toss to coat, adding as much of the reserved water as needed to help the sauce coat the noodles nicely. Serve on warm dishes. Serves 4.

PASTA "RISOTTO" WITH MUSHROOMS AND FONTINA

· 2 tablespoons unsalted butter

· 2 tablespoons olive oil

· 1 pound mushrooms,
halved if large, then sliced

· 1 teaspoon minced fresh thyme

· Salt and freshly ground
black pepper

· 1 pound dried rosmarino
or orzo pasta

· Approximately 5 cups
hot chicken stock
(or part stock / part water)

· ¼ pound Fontina Val d'Aosta
cheese, grated

· 2 tablespoons minced parsley

· ⅔ cup freshly grated
Parmesan cheese

COOKING RICE-SHAPED ROSMARINO PASTA BY THE RISOTTO METHOD—SIMMERING IT IN HOT LIQUID ADDED A LITTLE AT A TIME—YIELDS A CREAMY RESULT NOT UNLIKE A TRUE RISOTTO MADE WITH RICE. I LIKE TO STIR IN WELL-BROWNED MUSHROOMS AT THE END, ALONG WITH BUTTERY FONTINA CHEESE AND PARMESAN. ASK A GOOD CHEESE MERCHANT FOR FONTINA VAL D'AOSTA IMPORTED FROM ITALY.

ROSMARINO MEANS "ROSEMARY," AND INDEED THIS RICE-SHAPED PASTA RESEMBLES A ROSEMARY LEAF. DEPENDING ON THE MANUFACTURER, THE GRAINS ARE ABOUT THE SAME SIZE AS ORZO, WHICH YOU CAN SUBSTITUTE.

Melt 1 tablespoon of the butter with 1 tablespoon of the oil in a 12-inch skillet over high heat. Add mushrooms and thyme, season with salt and pepper, and sauté until mushrooms are cooked through and nicely browned, 5 to 10 minutes. Set aside and keep warm.

Heat remaining 1 tablespoon each butter and oil in a 6- to 8-quart saucepan over moderate heat. Add pasta and stir to coat with fat. Cook, stirring, for a minute or two to heat the pasta. Begin adding hot stock ¾ cup at a time, as if making risotto. Cook, stirring occasionally, until liquid is absorbed, then add more liquid. Adjust heat to maintain a steady simmer. Pasta should absorb about 4½ cups of liquid and be al dente in about 11 minutes. Use the remaining ½ cup stock if mixture looks too dry. It should have the moist and slightly creamy texture of a risotto.

Stir in mushrooms and Fontina. Cover, remove from heat and let stand 3 minutes. Uncover and stir in parsley and half of the Parmesan. Taste and adjust seasoning. Transfer to warm bowls and top with the remaining Parmesan. Serves 4.

GEMELLI WITH MUSHROOMS AND TOMATO

GEMELLI AREN'T EASY TO FIND, BUT THEY'RE ONE OF MY FAVORITE SHAPES BECAUSE THEY HOLD A TOMATO SAUCE SO NICELY. DELVERDE, AN ITALIAN MANUFACTURER, PACKAGES GEMELLI THAT LOOK ALMOST LIKE SHORT CINNAMON STICKS, BUT INSTEAD OF CURLING IN ONE DIRECTION, THEY CURL ONE WAY AND THEN THE OTHER TO MAKE AN S SHAPE. OTHER MANUFACTURERS' GEMELLI LOOK LIKE TWO SPAGHETTI STRANDS SPIRALED TOGETHER.

I HAVE OCCASIONALLY USED FRESH WILD MUSHROOMS FOR SOME OR ALL OF THE MUSHROOMS IN THIS DISH. MOST WILD MUSHROOMS NEED TO COOK SLOWLY, HOWEVER; STEW THEM GENTLY IN BUTTER OR OIL UNTIL THEY ARE TENDER, THEN COMBINE WITH THE TOMATO SAUCE. YOU CAN ALSO OMIT THE MUSHROOMS ENTIRELY; THIS RICH, ROSEMARY-SCENTED TOMATO SAUCE IS TASTY ENOUGH TO STAND ALONE.

· 5 tablespoons olive oil

· 3 to 4 ounces pancetta, minced

· 4 cloves garlic, minced

· ½ teaspoon minced fresh rosemary

· 2 cups strained canned tomatoes (pages 21–22)

· Salt and freshly ground black pepper

· 1 pound mushrooms, halved if large, then sliced

· 2 tablespoons minced parsley

· 1 pound dried gemelli ("twins"), fusilli or penne rigate (ridged tubes)

· ⅔ cup freshly grated Parmesan cheese

Combine 2 tablespoons of the olive oil, the pancetta, garlic and rosemary in a 12-inch skillet. Cook over moderately low heat, stirring occasionally, until pancetta just starts to crisp, 3 to 5 minutes. Add tomatoes to skillet. Bring to a simmer, adjust heat to maintain a simmer and cook until sauce is thick and tasty, about 15 minutes. Season to taste with salt and pepper. Transfer to a bowl.

Heat remaining 3 tablespoons oil in a 12-inch skillet over high heat. When oil is hot, add mushrooms and season with salt and pepper. Sauté, stirring occasionally, until they are nicely browned in spots and any liquid they release has evaporated, about 5 minutes. Add reserved tomato sauce and parsley and stir to blend.

Cook pasta in a large pot of boiling salted water until al dente. Just before it is done, reheat sauce gently. Drain pasta, reserving about ½ cup of the cooking water. Transfer pasta to a large warm bowl. Add sauce and toss. Add half of the cheese and toss again, adding a little of the reserved cooking water as needed to thin the sauce. Serve immediately on warm dishes, topping each portion with a little of the remaining cheese. Serves 4.

FETTUCCINE WITH MUSHROOMS AND FRIED SAGE

FRESH SAGE LEAVES TURN CRISP AND BRITTLE WHEN FRIED SLOWLY IN BUTTER. SCATTER THEM OVER PASTA WITH BUTTER-BROWNED MUSHROOMS TO MAKE A PRETTY CRACKLING GARNISH. IT IS IMPORTANT HERE TO USE GOOD-QUALITY STOCK—PREFERABLY HOMEMADE—BECAUSE YOU ARE GOING TO CONCENTRATE IT TO MAKE YOUR SAUCE.

· 4 tablespoons unsalted butter

· 1 tablespoon olive oil

· 48 large fresh sage leaves

· 2 pounds mushrooms, halved if large, then sliced

· Salt and freshly ground black pepper

· 1½ cups homemade veal stock or best-quality canned beef broth

· 1 pound fresh fettuccine

Melt 2 tablespoons of the butter with the oil in a 12-inch skillet over moderately low heat. Add sage leaves and fry slowly, turning occasionally, until they are crisp, 7 to 8 minutes. Lower heat if necessary to keep butter from burning. Transfer with tongs to paper towels to drain. Pour off fat in skillet and reserve.

Preheat oven to lowest setting. Raise heat under skillet to high. When skillet is very hot, add mushrooms. (Don't worry: they won't stick because they will quickly render their juices.) Cut remaining 2 tablespoons butter into small pieces and add to skillet. Season mushrooms highly with salt and pepper. Sauté over high heat until all the mushroom juices have evaporated and the mushrooms begin to sizzle and brown, about 15 minutes. Transfer them to a large warm bowl and place in oven.

Add stock to skillet and stir with a wooden spoon to scrape up any particles clinging to pan bottom. Simmer over high heat until stock is reduced by half, then lower heat and keep warm while you cook the pasta.

Cook pasta in a large pot of boiling salted water until al dente. Drain. Transfer to skillet. Add the reserved sage-flavored butter. Toss to coat noodles with stock and butter. Transfer noodles to the bowl containing the mushrooms and toss again. Serve immediately on warm dishes, topping each portion with some of the sage leaves. Serves 4.

Mushrooms

PEAS / PEPPERS / POTATOES

PEAS

- Gnocchi with Peas, Green Onions and Basil
- Farfalle with Peas, Tarragon and Cream
- Linguine with Peas and Radicchio
- Linguine with Peas, Prosciutto and Mint

PEPPERS

- Linguine with Mixed Sweet Peppers, Feta and Oregano
- Fusilli with Roasted Red Pepper Cream
- Spaghetti with Sweet Peppers

POTATOES

- Whole-Wheat Spaghettini with Potatoes, Pancetta and Arugula
- Linguine with New Potatoes and Pesto

PEAS

I ADORE FRESH ENGLISH PEAS BUT THEY ARE FRUSTRATING. EVEN IN EARLY SUMMER—PEAK PEA SEASON—THE MARKETS OFTEN HAVE ONLY PEAS THAT ARE OLD, OVERGROWN AND NO LONGER SWEET. I SOMETIMES GROW MY OWN AND DO FIND GOOD ONES AT FARMERS' MARKETS, BUT MOST OF THE TIME WHAT THE CONVENTIONAL MARKETS OFFER ISN'T WORTH BUYING. WHEN YOU CAN FIND GREAT PEAS, GET YOUR FILL OF THEM IN THESE PASTA DISHES. AT OTHER TIMES, A PREMIUM BRAND OF FROZEN PETITE PEAS IS A FINE SUBSTITUTE. ✐ WHEN BUYING FRESH ENGLISH PEAS, LOOK FOR SMOOTH, UNBLEMISHED PODS THAT ARE FILLED BUT NOT BULGING. LARGE PEAS WILL PROBABLY BE STARCHY. TRY TO BUY PEAS THE DAY YOU INTEND TO USE THEM; IF YOU CAN'T, REFRIGERATE THEM IN A PERFORATED PLASTIC BAG.

GNOCCHI WITH PEAS, GREEN ONIONS AND BASIL

HERE'S ANOTHER ONE-POT PASTA DISH, WHERE PASTA AND VEGETABLES COOK TOGETHER. IF YOUR PEAS ARE OF MODERATE SIZE, THEY SHOULD COOK IN ABOUT THE SAME TIME IT TAKES TO COOK THE GNOCCHI. IF YOUR PEAS ARE ON THE SMALL SIDE, ADD THEM TO THE POT A FEW MINUTES AFTER STARTING THE PASTA.

· 4 tablespoons unsalted butter, in 8 pieces

· ⅔ cup finely minced green onions (scallions), white and pale green parts only

· 3 cups shelled peas (about 3 pounds unshelled)

· 1 pound dried gnocchi

· 24 fresh basil leaves

· ¼ cup minced parsley

· Salt and freshly ground black pepper

· 1 cup freshly grated Parmesan cheese

✐ Preheat oven to lowest setting. Put butter and green onions in a large serving bowl and place in oven.

✐ Bring a large pot of salted water—at least 5 quarts—to a boil. Add peas and pasta and cook until pasta is al dente. Just before the pasta is ready, chop the basil leaves.

✐ Drain the pasta and peas, reserving about ½ cup of the cooking water. Add pasta and peas to warmed bowl along with basil, parsley and salt and pepper to taste. Toss well. Add cheese and toss again, adding some of the reserved cooking water as needed to moisten the pasta. Serve immediately on warm dishes. Serves 4.

FARFALLE WITH PEAS, TARRAGON AND CREAM

SWEET PEAS CLOAKED IN CREAM MAKE A LOVELY PASTA SAUCE THAT WOULD BE AS TASTY ON FRESH LINGUINE AS ON THE DRIED FARFALLE SUGGESTED HERE.

- *3 tablespoons unsalted butter*
- *1½ cups minced green onions (scallions), white and pale green parts only*
- *1 cup heavy cream*
- *1 cup chicken stock*
- *2 teaspoons minced fresh tarragon*
- *Salt and freshly ground black pepper*
- *2½ cups freshly shelled English peas (about 2½ pounds unshelled) or frozen petite peas*
- *1 pound dried farfalle ("butterflies")*
- *2 ounces prosciutto di Parma, finely minced*
- *½ cup freshly grated Parmesan cheese*

❧ Melt butter in a 12-inch skillet over moderately low heat. Add green onions and sauté until softened, about 3 minutes. Add cream, stock, tarragon and salt and pepper to taste. Bring to a simmer and adjust heat to maintain a simmer. Cook a few minutes until reduced to a saucelike consistency. It should be thick enough to coat the pasta nicely, but remember that the cheese will thicken it further. Keep warm.

❧ Boil fresh peas in a large quantity of salted water until tender, 5 to 8 minutes, or cook frozen peas according to package directions. Drain. Add peas to sauce.

❧ Cook pasta in a large pot of boiling salted water until al dente. Just before pasta is done, add prosciutto to sauce. Drain pasta, reserving about ½ cup of the cooking water. Transfer to a large warm bowl. Add sauce and toss gently. Add cheese and toss again, adding some of the reserved water if needed to thin the sauce. Serve immediately on warm dishes. Serves 4.

LINGUINE WITH PEAS AND RADICCHIO

RADICCHIO LOSES ITS DRAMATIC COLOR WHEN COOKED, BUT THIS IS STILL A PRETTY DISH, WITH THE PEAS AND PARSLEY CONTRASTING WITH THE DARK RADICCHIO RIBBONS. ADDING THE GREEN ONIONS AT THE LAST MINUTE GIVES THE PASTA A FLAVOR BOOST.

- 4 ounces pancetta, minced

- 3 tablespoons unsalted butter

- 2 small cloves garlic, minced

- 1½ cups freshly shelled English peas (about 1½ pounds unshelled) or frozen petite peas

- 1 cup chicken stock

- 6 ounces radicchio, thinly sliced

- Salt and freshly ground black pepper

- 1 pound fresh linguine

- ½ cup minced green onions (scallions), white and pale green parts only

- ¼ cup minced parsley

❧ Combine pancetta and 1 tablespoon butter in a 12-inch skillet. Cook over moderately low heat, stirring occasionally, until pancetta begins to crisp, 3 to 5 minutes. Add garlic and sauté 1 minute to release its fragrance. Add peas and stock. Bring to a simmer, adjust heat to maintain a simmer and cook until peas are tender, 6 to 8 minutes for fresh peas and 4 to 5 minutes for frozen peas. Add a little hot water if stock reduces too much; you want to have about ¼ cup of liquid left in the skillet when the peas are done. Add radicchio and remove from heat. Season with salt and pepper and toss to wilt radicchio; it will wilt in the residual heat.

❧ Put remaining 2 tablespoons butter in a large bowl and place in a warm oven. Cook pasta in a large pot of boiling salted water until al dente. Drain and transfer to the warmed bowl. Toss to coat with butter. Add contents of skillet, green onions and parsley. Toss. Serve on warm dishes. Serves 4.

LINGUINE WITH PEAS, PROSCIUTTO AND MINT

FRESH OR FROZEN BABY LIMA BEANS WOULD ALSO BE APPEALING HERE, IN ADDITION TO OR IN PLACE OF THE PEAS.

❂ Melt 4 tablespoons of the butter in a 12-inch skillet over moderate heat. Add green onions and sauté until softened, about 3 minutes. Add peas and stock. Bring to a simmer, cover and reduce heat to maintain a simmer. Cook until peas are tender, 6 to 8 minutes for fresh peas and 4 to 5 minutes for frozen peas.

❂ Cook pasta in a large pot of boiling salted water until al dente. Just before pasta is done, reheat peas gently and stir in mint, prosciutto and salt and pepper to taste. Drain pasta and transfer to a large warm bowl. Add the remaining 2 tablespoons butter, in small pieces, and toss. Add contents of skillet and toss again. Serve immediately on warm dishes. Serves 4.

· 6 tablespoons unsalted butter

· 1½ cups sliced green onions (scallions), white and pale green parts only

· 3 cups freshly shelled English peas (about 3 pounds unshelled) or frozen petite peas

· 1 cup chicken stock

· 1 pound fresh linguine

· 3 tablespoons chopped fresh mint

· 3 ounces prosciutto di Parma, minced

· Salt and freshly ground black pepper

PEPPERS

PEPPERS LATE SUMMER IS THE HEIGHT OF THE SEASON FOR SWEET BELL PEPPERS. GREEN PEPPERS LEFT ON THE PLANT TO RIPEN IN THE SUMMER HEAT TURN RED, YELLOW OR ORANGE, DEPENDING ON THE VARIETY, AND DEVELOP INTENSE FLAVOR AND SWEETNESS. THEY SEEM TO TASTE BETTER, AND CERTAINLY COST LESS, THAN THE PEPPERS SHIPPED IN FROM FARAWAY WARM CLIMATES DURING OUR OFF-SEASON. ⬤ IT IS IMPORTANT TO SELECT PEPPERS THAT FEEL HEAVY FOR THEIR SIZE; HEAVINESS INDICATES THAT THEY ARE THICK-WALLED AND MEATY. THEY SHOULD ALSO HAVE DEEP, RICH COLOR AND NO SOFT OR MOLDY SPOTS. FOR EVEN ROASTING AND EASY SLICING, BUY THE MOST UNIFORM PEPPERS YOU CAN FIND. ⬤ PEPPERS DON'T APPRECIATE COLD. IF YOU CAN'T USE THEM IMMEDIATELY, STORE THEM IN A PERFORATED PLASTIC BAG IN THE WARMEST PART OF THE REFRIGERATOR—USUALLY THE DOOR STORAGE AREA. ⬤ TO ROAST PEPPERS, PLACE THEM UNDER A PREHEATED BROILER, ON A GAS BURNER OR ON A CHARCOAL GRILL, TURNING TO BLISTER AND BLACKEN ALL SIDES. PUT THE PEPPERS IN A PAPER BAG TO STEAM. WHEN COOL ENOUGH TO HANDLE, PEEL THEM AND REMOVE SEEDS, STEMS AND RIBS. CAREFULLY REMOVE ALL TRACES OF BLACK SKIN, BUT DO NOT RINSE THE PEPPERS OR YOU'LL WASH AWAY THE FLAVOR. CUT AS DIRECTED IN INDIVIDUAL RECIPES.

LINGUINE WITH MIXED SWEET PEPPERS, FETA AND OREGANO

YOU CAN USE PEPPERS ALL OF ONE COLOR, OF COURSE, BUT MIXED COLORS ARE PRETTIER. I RECOMMEND BUYING FETA IMPORTED FROM GREECE OR BULGARIA, WHERE IT IS MADE FROM SHEEP'S OR GOAT'S MILK. DOMESTIC FETA IS USUALLY MADE FROM COW'S MILK AND DOES NOT HAVE AN AUTHENTIC FLAVOR.

· 1 large red bell pepper

· 1 large green bell pepper

· 1 large yellow bell pepper

· ¼ cup olive oil

· 4 cloves garlic, minced

· 1 pound ripe plum tomatoes, peeled and seeded (page 22), then chopped

⬤ Halve the peppers through the stem end. Cut away stem, core and white ribs. Slice peppers thinly. Heat olive oil in a 12-inch skillet over moderate heat. Add garlic and sauté 1 minute to release its fragrance. Add tomatoes, raise heat to moderately high and cook, stirring constantly, until tomatoes collapse and form a thick sauce, about 10 minutes. Add water as necessary to keep tomatoes from sticking. When sauce is thick and nearly smooth, stir in peppers, oregano and salt to taste. Cover, reduce heat to moderately low and cook until peppers are tender but not completely soft, 15 to 20 minutes. Uncover and check occasionally to make sure they are not burning; they should not need additional liquid.

- 2 teaspoons minced fresh oregano

- Salt

- 1 pound dried linguine

- 6 ounces Greek or Bulgarian feta cheese, crumbled

✎ Cook pasta in a large pot of boiling salted water until al dente. Transfer with tongs to a large warm bowl, allowing some of the water to cling to the noodles. Add contents of skillet and toss. Add feta and toss again, adding a few

tablespoons of hot pasta water as necessary to make the sauce a little creamy. Serve immediately on warm dishes. Serves 4.

FUSILLI WITH ROASTED RED PEPPER CREAM

ROASTING RED PEPPERS INTENSIFIES THEIR SWEETNESS AND SOFTENS THEM ENOUGH TO PURÉE FOR SAUCE. ENRICHED WITH JUST A LITTLE CREAM AND PERKED UP WITH CAYENNE, THE SAUCE IS SO GOOD THAT IT TAKES SOME WILLPOWER TO RESIST EATING IT RIGHT OUT OF THE SKILLET. DEPENDING ON THE SIZE OF YOUR PEPPERS, THIS RECIPE MAY YIELD A LITTLE BIT MORE THAN YOU NEED; HOLD BACK A FEW TABLESPOONS WHEN YOU'RE SAUCING THE PASTA TO MAKE SURE THAT YOU NEED IT ALL.

- 1 tablespoon olive oil

- 3 ounces pancetta, minced

- ⅔ cup minced yellow onion

- 2 large cloves garlic, minced

- 2 large, heavy red bell peppers, roasted, peeled, seeded and diced (page 110)

- 1 cup chicken stock

- ¼ cup heavy cream

- Salt and cayenne pepper

- 1 pound dried fusilli

- 1 cup freshly grated Parmesan cheese

- 2 tablespoons minced parsley

✎ Heat olive oil and pancetta in a 12-inch skillet over moderately low heat. Cook, stirring occasionally, until pancetta begins to crisp, 3 to 5 minutes. Add onion and sauté until softened, about 10 minutes. Add garlic and sauté 1 minute to release its fragrance. Add bell pepper, stock and cream and bring to a simmer. Reduce heat to low and simmer 5 minutes.

✎ Purée sauce in a food processor until almost completely smooth (a little texture is nice). Return to skillet and season with salt and cayenne to taste. Just before pasta is ready, reheat gently.

✎ Cook pasta in a large pot of boiling salted water until al dente. Drain, reserving about ½ cup of the cooking water. Transfer pasta to a large warm bowl. Add sauce (see introduction) and toss to coat. Add ½ cup of the Parmesan and toss again, adding as much of the reserved water as needed to help the sauce coat the noodles nicely. Serve immediately on warm dishes. Top each serving with some of the remaining ½ cup Parmesan and the parsley. Serves 4.

SPAGHETTI WITH SWEET PEPPERS

✓†† 2-19

IN LATE SUMMER, MY LOCAL PRODUCE MARKETS DISPLAY GORGEOUS HEAPS OF CALIFORNIA BELL PEPPERS IN GREEN, RED AND GOLD. COOKED TOGETHER WITH THYME AND GARLIC, THEY MAKE A BEAUTIFUL PASTA SAUCE.

· 3 large or 4 medium red bell peppers

· 3 large or 4 medium yellow bell peppers

· 6 tablespoons olive oil

· 1 tablespoon minced fresh thyme

· Salt

· 6 cloves garlic, minced

· ¼ teaspoon hot red pepper flakes, or more to taste

· 1 pound dried spaghetti

· 3 tablespoons minced parsley

· Freshly grated pecorino romano cheese for passing

Halve the peppers through the stem end. Cut away stem, core and white ribs. Slice peppers thinly. Heat olive oil in a 12- to 14-inch skillet over moderate heat. Add peppers and thyme; season with salt and toss to coat with oil. Cover and cook until peppers are soft but not mushy, 15 to 20 minutes, adjusting heat so peppers stew briskly without burning. Uncover and stir occasionally. Stir in garlic and hot red pepper flakes about 5 minutes before peppers are done. Keep warm.

Cook pasta in a large pot of boiling salted water until al dente. Just before pasta is ready, transfer about ¼ cup of the hot pasta water to the skillet and stir to release any pepper juices adhering to the skillet. Transfer pasta with tongs to a warm bowl, allowing some water to cling to the noodles. Add contents of skillet and parsley and toss well. Serve immediately on warm dishes. Pass cheese at the table. Serves 4.

POTATOES

AN ODD VEGETABLE FOR A PASTA SAUCE? NOT IN ITALY. LIGURIANS—FROM THE REGION NEAR GENOA—DELIGHT IN PASTA WITH POTATOES AND PESTO; IN THE COLD VALTELLINA, NORTH OF MILAN, COOKS MAKE PIZZOCCHERI—BUCKWHEAT PASTA WITH POTATOES, CHARD AND CHEESE. IF YOU ARE STILL DOUBTFUL, PERHAPS THE FOLLOWING TWO DELICIOUS RECIPES WILL CHANGE YOUR MIND. ❡ ALTHOUGH SMALL RED-SKINNED POTATOES ARE HARVESTED THE YEAR AROUND, THEY SOMETIMES FEEL SPONGY, AS IF THEY'VE BEEN IN STORAGE TOO LONG. LOOK FOR FIRM POTATOES WITH NO SPROUTING AND KEEP THEM IN A COOL, DARK, DRY PLACE.

WHOLE-WHEAT SPAGHETTINI WITH POTATOES, PANCETTA AND ARUGULA

THIS SAUCE TAKES ALL OF 5 MINUTES TO MAKE—LESS TIME THAN IT TAKES TO COOK THE PASTA AND POTATOES. IT'S IMPORTANT TO USE A FULL-FLAVORED OLIVE OIL, WAXY POTATOES (THE KIND YOU USE FOR POTATO SALAD) AND YOUNG ARUGULA, WITHOUT THICK STEMS. I ALSO FIND THAT THIS DISH REQUIRES A GOOD DEAL OF SALT, PERHAPS BECAUSE IT HAS NO CHEESE.

- *½ cup extra virgin olive oil*
- *3 to 4 ounces pancetta, minced*
- *4 cloves garlic, minced*
- *¼ teaspoon hot red pepper flakes*
- *½ pound arugula, preferably young, small leaves (if large, chop coarsely)*
- *Salt*
- *1 pound waxy red-skinned potatoes, unpeeled*
- *1 pound dried whole-wheat spaghettini or spaghetti*

❡ Bring a large pot of salted water—at least 5 quarts—to a boil. Combine 1 tablespoon of the olive oil and the pancetta in a 12-inch skillet. Cook over moderately low heat, stirring occasionally, until it just begins to crisp, 3 to 5 minutes. Add garlic and hot red pepper flakes and sauté 1 minute to release garlic fragrance. Add arugula and toss with tongs to coat with oil; cook just until arugula barely wilts, a minute or so. Season with salt. Keep warm.

❡ Preheat oven to lowest setting. If potatoes are small, halve them lengthwise. If they are large, quarter lengthwise. Cut crosswise into slices about ⅛ inch thick. When water boils, add potatoes, stir and cover. When water returns to a boil, add pasta.

❡ Put remaining 7 tablespoons olive oil in a large bowl with a generous pinch of salt. Place in oven to warm. When pasta is al dente, drain, reserving about ½ cup of the cooking water. Add pasta and potatoes to warmed bowl and toss to coat with oil. Add contents of skillet and enough reserved pasta water to make the noodles moist and shiny. Toss gently but well. Serve immediately on warm dishes. Serves 4.

LINGUINE WITH NEW POTATOES AND PESTO

YOU SEE THIS DISH ON RESTAURANT MENUS IN AND AROUND GENOA, ESPECIALLY IN THE SIMPLE SEAFOOD RESTAURANTS THAT LINE THE LIGURIAN COAST. MOST ITALIAN COOKS USE TRENETTE—FRESH RIBBON PASTA SLICED NARROWER THAN LINGUINE—BUT I LIKE THE FIRMNESS OF DRIED LINGUINE HERE. I ALSO PREFER TO USE WAXY NEW POTATOES BECAUSE THEY HOLD THEIR SHAPE WHEN BOILED; TRADITIONALISTS USE RUSSET-TYPE POTATOES, WHICH GIVE A STARCHIER RESULT. TRY THE TWO KINDS YOURSELF AND SEE WHICH YOU PREFER.

IT'S NOT EASY TO GIVE A PRECISE MEASUREMENT FOR BASIL LEAVES. SOME ARE BIG, SOME SMALL. HERE'S WHAT I DO: AFTER WASHING AND DRYING THE LEAVES IN A SALAD SPINNER, I TEAR THE BIG ONES INTO THREE OR FOUR PIECES, SMALLER ONES IN HALF OR NOT AT ALL. THEN I PACK THE MEASURING CUP FIRMLY BUT NOT TIGHTLY.

For the pesto:
- *¼ cup pine nuts*
- *1½ cups fresh basil leaves (see introduction)*
- *2 cloves garlic, thinly sliced*
- *½ cup olive oil*
- *3 tablespoons freshly grated Parmesan cheese*
- *3 tablespoons freshly grated Pecorino romano cheese*
- *Salt*

- *1 pound red-skinned new potatoes*
- *1 pound dried linguine*

To make pesto, preheat oven to 325°F. Spread pine nuts on a baking sheet or in a pie pan and toast until golden brown, 10 to 15 minutes, shaking pan occasionally so nuts brown evenly. Let cool.

In a food processor, combine pine nuts, basil leaves and garlic. Process until well chopped, scraping down sides of bowl once or twice. With motor running, add olive oil through the feed tube in a steady stream; stop machine and scrape down sides of bowl once or twice. Stop processing before mixture is completely smooth; pesto should have a little texture to it. Transfer to a bowl. Stir in cheeses and salt to taste. Don't scrimp on the salt or the final dish will taste bland. Press plastic wrap against the surface to prevent discoloring.

If potatoes are small, halve them lengthwise. If they are large, quarter them lengthwise. Cut crosswise into slices about ⅛ inch thick. Bring a large pot of well-salted water to a boil. Add potatoes, stir, then cover pot. When water returns to a boil, add pasta. Cook at a rolling boil until al dente, stirring occasionally.

Just before pasta is ready, put pesto in a large warm bowl and whisk in 4 to 6 tablespoons of the hot pasta water— enough to give the pesto a saucelike consistency. Drain pasta and potatoes, reserving about ½ cup of the water. Transfer pasta and potatoes to the warm bowl and toss gently to coat. Add some of the reserved hot water if needed to help pesto coat the noodles nicely. Serve immediately on warm dishes. Serves 4.

SPINACH / SQUASHES

SPINACH

FRESH SPINACH ADDS BEAUTIFUL GREEN COLOR, DISTINCTIVE FLAVOR AND A POWERFUL PACKAGE OF NUTRIENTS TO PASTA SAUCES. WHAT'S MORE, IT IS NOW WIDELY AVAILABLE THE YEAR AROUND— EVEN, IN SOME MARKETS, ALREADY WASHED AND DRIED. WHEN BUYING FRESH SPINACH, AVOID BUNCHES THAT CONTAIN ANY YELLOWING OR DECAYING LEAVES. IF POSSIBLE, CHOOSE YOUNG SPINACH WITH SMALL LEAVES AND THIN STEMS; OLDER SPINACH WITH THICK STEMS WILL BE TOUGHER AND STRONGER TASTING. ✇ BEFORE STORING, REMOVE ANY BANDS AROUND THE SPINACH. WASH AND DRAIN WELL, THEN WRAP IN PAPER TOWELS OR A DISH TOWEL AND SLIP INSIDE A PLASTIC BAG. REFRIGERATE AND USE AS SOON AS POSSIBLE.

LINGUINE WITH SPINACH PESTO

WHEN BASIL ISN'T AVAILABLE FOR TRADITIONAL PESTO, SPINACH MAKES A FINE SUBSTITUTE. OF COURSE IT DOESN'T HAVE THE PUNGENT AROMA OF BASIL PESTO, BUT THIS VERSION IS TASTY IN ITS OWN RIGHT.

- ¼ cup pine nuts
- ⅓ pound spinach leaves, thick stems removed (from about ½ pound untrimmed spinach), carefully washed and dried
- 1 clove garlic, thinly sliced
- ½ cup olive oil
- ½ cup freshly grated Parmesan cheese, plus additional Parmesan cheese for passing
- Salt and freshly ground black pepper
- 1 pound fresh linguine

✇ Preheat oven to 325°F. Spread pine nuts on a baking sheet or in a pie pan and toast until golden brown, 10 to 15 minutes, shaking pan occasionally so nuts brown evenly. Let cool.

✇ In food processor, combine spinach leaves, garlic and pine nuts. Process until well chopped, scraping down sides of bowl once or twice. With motor running, add oil through the feed tube in a steady stream. Stop and scrape down sides of bowl once or twice. When mixture is smooth or nearly so (a little texture is okay), transfer to a bowl and stir in ½ cup Parmesan and salt and pepper to taste.

✇ Cook pasta in a large pot of boiling salted water until al dente. Near the end of the cooking time, remove about ½ cup of the hot water. Whisk ¼ cup hot water into the pesto, then transfer the pesto to a large warm bowl. Drain pasta and add to bowl. Toss well, adding a little more hot water if needed to help the sauce coat the noodles nicely. Serve immediately on warm dishes. Pass additional Parmesan at the table. Serves 4.

BAKED RIGATONI WITH SPINACH AND FONTINA

WHAT "MAKES" THIS DISH IS THE INCOMPARABLE FONTINA VAL D'AOSTA CHEESE FROM ITALY.
IT HAS A BUTTERY TEXTURE AND A PUNGENT, ALMOST EARTHY AROMA THAT REMINDS ME OF
WHITE TRUFFLES. A GOOD CHEESE MERCHANT WILL HAVE IT. DON'T SETTLE FOR ANY OF THE
LESSER CHEESES WITH SIMILAR NAMES.

- 3 tablespoons unsalted butter
- ¼ cup all-purpose flour
- 3 cups milk
- ½ small yellow onion, sliced
- 1 clove garlic, halved
- 1 bay leaf
- Salt and freshly ground black pepper
- 1 pound fresh spinach leaves, thick stems removed (from about 1½ pounds untrimmed spinach)
- 1½ cups grated Fontina Val d'Aosta cheese (about ⅓ pound)
- 1 pound dried rigatoni
- ⅓ to ½ cup freshly grated Parmesan cheese

Preheat oven to 350°F. To make a béchamel sauce, melt butter in a heavy-bottomed, 2-quart saucepan over moderately low heat. Add flour and whisk to blend. Cook, whisking constantly, for a minute or two, then add milk, onion, garlic and bay leaf. Bring to a simmer, whisking often, then reduce heat to lowest setting and cook, whisking occasionally, 20 minutes to draw the flavors out of the seasonings. Season with salt and pepper. Strain sauce through a fine-mesh sieve into a large bowl, pressing on the onion and garlic with the back of a spoon to extract their flavor.

Wash spinach carefully in a sink filled with cold water. Transfer spinach to a 12-inch skillet with just the water clinging to the leaves. Cover and cook over moderate heat until leaves are just wilted, about 3 minutes, tossing once or twice with tongs so leaves wilt evenly. Transfer to a sieve and place under cold running water until cool. Drain well and squeeze dry between your hands. Chop medium-fine.

Stir spinach into béchamel sauce. Stir in Fontina. Season with salt and pepper.

Cook pasta in a large pot of boiling salted water for 8 minutes. It will taste underdone, but it will continue to cook in the oven. Drain pasta well, then stir into spinach sauce. Transfer the mixture to a baking dish measuring approximately 14 by 10 by 3 inches. Dust surface lightly with Parmesan; use ⅓ to ½ cup, depending on the surface area of your dish. Bake until sauce starts to bubble around the edges, 15 to 20 minutes. Serve immediately on warm dishes. Serves 4 to 6.

SPAGHETTI WITH SPINACH, PANCETTA AND EGG

THE INGREDIENTS THAT ARE SO COMPATIBLE IN A WARM SPINACH SALAD ALSO WORK TOGETHER AS A PASTA SAUCE. HERE, AS IN SPAGHETTI CARBONARA, THE SAUCE DERIVES FROM RAW EGG PARTIALLY COOKED BY HOT PASTA. I LIKE THE TASTE OF COARSELY CRACKED BLACK PEPPER HERE—GROUND FRESH FROM A MILL OR POUNDED IN A MORTAR.

· 1 pound spinach leaves, thick stems removed (from about 1½ pounds untrimmed spinach)

· 4 eggs

· ¾ cup freshly grated Parmesan cheese

· Salt and freshly cracked black pepper

· 1 tablespoon olive oil

· 1 tablespoon unsalted butter

· 4 ounces pancetta, minced

· 2 large cloves garlic, minced

· 1 pound dried spaghetti

❂ Wash spinach carefully in a sink filled with cold water. Transfer spinach to a 12-inch skillet with just the water clinging to the leaves. Cover and cook over moderate heat until leaves are just wilted, about 3 minutes, tossing once or twice with tongs so leaves wilt evenly. Transfer to a sieve and place under cold running water until cool. Drain well and squeeze dry between your hands. Chop medium-fine.

❂ Whisk eggs in a large serving bowl. Add cheese and salt and pepper to taste. Whisk to blend and set aside.

❂ Combine olive oil, butter, pancetta and garlic in a 12-inch skillet. Cook over moderately low heat, stirring occasionally, until pancetta just begins to crisp, 3 to 5 minutes. Add spinach and stir to coat with fat. Season with salt and pepper. Keep warm.

❂ Cook pasta in a large pot of boiling salted water until al dente. Transfer spaghetti with tongs to the bowl containing the egg mixture, leaving a little water clinging to the noodles. Immediately toss to coat spaghetti with egg mixture, which will "cook" in the pasta's heat. If needed, add a little hot pasta water to thin the sauce. Add contents of skillet and toss again. Serve immediately on warm dishes. Serves 4.

BAKED CONCHIGLIONE WITH SPINACH-RICOTTA FILLING

THIS IS A PRETTY SIGHT AFTER IT'S BAKED, WITH THE RICH TOMATO SAUCE BUBBLING AROUND THE PLUMP STUFFED SHELLS. BRING IT STRAIGHT TO THE TABLE AND SERVE IT FROM THE BAKING DISH.

YOU CAN USE THE SAME FILLING FOR CANNELLONI, BUT IT'S MORE EYE-APPEALING IN THE SHELLS BECAUSE THEY HOLD THEIR FILLING FACE UP. I ALWAYS BOIL A FEW EXTRA SHELLS (MORE THAN THE 20 REQUIRED) TO ALLOW FOR BREAKAGE. CHOOSE A MOZZARELLA THAT IS FIRM ENOUGH TO GRATE; A VERY FRESH, MOIST WHOLE-MILK MOZZARELLA IS TOO WET FOR THIS FILLING.

- ½ pound spinach leaves, thick stems removed (from about ¾ pound untrimmed spinach)

- 2 cloves garlic, minced

- ½ pound whole-milk ricotta cheese (about 1 cup)

- ½ pound whole-milk mozzarella cheese, coarsely grated

- 1 egg, lightly beaten

- 1 tablespoon finely minced fresh basil

- Salt and freshly ground black pepper

- 20 conchiglione ("jumbo shells"), about ½ pound total weight

- 2 teaspoons olive oil

- 1½ cups Summer Tomato Sauce (page 140)

- ½ cup freshly grated pecorino romano cheese

✐ Preheat oven to 375°F. Wash spinach carefully in a sink filled with cold water. Transfer spinach to a 10-inch skillet with just the water clinging to the leaves. Cover and cook over moderate heat until leaves are just wilted, about 3 minutes, tossing once or twice with tongs so leaves wilt evenly. Transfer wilted leaves to a sieve and place under cold running water until cool. Drain well and squeeze dry between your hands. Chop finely.

✐ In a bowl, combine spinach, garlic, ricotta, mozzarella, egg, basil and salt and pepper to taste. Mix well.

✐ Cook shells in a large pot of boiling salted water. Drain them when they are about a minute shy of being done (they will continue to cook in the oven). Transfer shells to a bowl and toss with olive oil to keep them from sticking together.

✐ Put half the tomato sauce on the bottom of a shallow baking dish just large enough to hold the shells in one layer. Fill each shell with a heaping tablespoon of stuffing. You should have just enough stuffing to fill 20 shells. Arrange the shells in the dish. Spoon remaining sauce over and around the shells. Top with pecorino cheese. Cover with aluminum foil and bake until bubbling hot, 30 to 40 minutes. Serve directly from baking dish on warm dishes. Serves 4.

FUSILLI WITH SPINACH AND RICOTTA SAUCE

THIS CREAMY SAUCE MELTS INTO A BEAUTIFUL GREEN CLOAK ON HOT PASTA. I LIKE TO USE
FUSILLI HERE BECAUSE THE GROOVES TRAP THE SAUCE, BUT SPAGHETTI, PENNE RIGATE
(RIDGED TUBES) OR RUOTE ("WHEELS") WOULD WORK, TOO.

· 2 bunches spinach (to yield
¾ pound trimmed leaves)

· 1½ tablespoons
unsalted butter

· 1 large or 2 small cloves
garlic, minced

· ½ cup whole-milk
ricotta cheese

· ½ cup freshly grated
Parmesan cheese, plus additional Parmesan cheese
for passing

· Salt and freshly ground
black pepper

· 1 pound dried fusilli

With a large knife, slice across spinach bunches to separate leaves from stems. Swish leaves well in a sink filled with cold water, lifting them out to leave the dirt behind; drain and refill sink and repeat washing if necessary. Weigh out ¾ pound leaves; reserve the rest for salad or another use.

Put the spinach leaves in a 12-inch skillet with just the water clinging to them. Cover and cook over moderate heat until leaves are just wilted, about 3 minutes, tossing once or twice with tongs so leaves wilt evenly. Transfer wilted leaves to a sieve and place under cold running water until cool. Drain well and squeeze between your hands to remove excess water. The spinach does not need to be thoroughly dry.

Melt butter in a small skillet over low heat. Add garlic and sauté 1 minute to release its fragrance. Put spinach, garlic and butter in food processor and process to chop. Add ricotta and process until smooth, stopping machine to scrape down sides of bowl once or twice. Transfer to a bowl. Stir in ½ cup Parmesan and season generously with salt and pepper.

Cook pasta in a large pot of boiling salted water until al dente. Drain, reserving 1 cup water. Transfer to a large warm bowl. Add as much of the sauce as you like and toss to coat, adding reserved water as necessary to thin the sauce. (I find that I usually have a couple of tablespoons of sauce left over. Refrigerate any remaining sauce and spread it on toasted croutons the next day.) Serve pasta immediately in warm dishes and pass additional Parmesan at the table. Serves 4.

SQUASHES

BOTH THIN-SKINNED SUMMER ZUCCHINI AND HARD-SHELLED WINTER SQUASHES ARE WELCOME IN THE PASTA KITCHEN. ZUCCHINI CAN BE BROILED OR GRILLED WITH OLIVE OIL AND GARLIC; SIMMERED IN TOMATO SAUCE; OR BRAISED IN BUTTER WITH SPRING HERBS BEFORE TOSSING WITH PASTA. GREEN AND GOLDEN ZUCCHINI TOGETHER MAKE A PARTICULARLY PRETTY SAUCE, WHATEVER THE SEASONINGS. IN WINTER, I LIKE TO ADD DICED BUTTERNUT SQUASH AND LEEKS TO RICE-SHAPED PASTA. ✎ WHEN BUYING SUMMER SQUASHES (SUCH AS ZUCCHINI), CHOOSE SMALL ONES OVER LARGE ONES. SMALL ONES TEND TO HAVE A FIRM TEXTURE AND SWEET FLAVOR; LARGE ONES CAN BE WATERY AND BITTER. ZUCCHINI SHOULD HAVE SMOOTH, UNBLEMISHED SKIN AND NO SOFT SPOTS. STORE IN A PERFORATED PLASTIC BAG IN THE REFRIGERATOR. ✎ AMONG WINTER SQUASHES, BUTTERNUT IS MY FAVORITE BECAUSE IT HAS DENSE, SWEET FLESH AND IT IS EASY TO PEEL. HOWEVER, BUTTERCUP, KABOCHA OR DELICATA SQUASH WILL WORK IN THE RECIPE ON PAGE 129. BECAUSE WINTER SQUASHES ARE SUCH GOOD KEEPERS, THEY ARE USUALLY IN GOOD CONDITION AT THE MARKET. AVOID ANY THAT HAVE SOFT OR MOLDY SPOTS, OF COURSE; IF YOU ARE BUYING CUT SQUASH, IT SHOULD LOOK MOIST. AN UNCUT SQUASH WILL KEEP FOR WEEKS IN A COOL, DARK PLACE; IF CUT, HOWEVER, THE SQUASH SHOULD BE REFRIGERATED.

ZUCCHINI LINGUINE

SAVE THIS RECIPE FOR WHEN YOU FIND SMALL, SLENDER ZUCCHINI. THEY'LL HAVE THE FIRM TEXTURE AND SWEET FLAVOR THAT MAKE THEM WORTH FEATURING IN PASTA. YOU CAN BROIL THEM, AS DESCRIBED BELOW, OR IF YOU'RE NOT PRESSED FOR TIME, FIRE UP THE CHARCOAL GRILL AND COOK THEM OVER MEDIUM-HOT COALS.

· *2 pounds small zucchini, about 1 inch in diameter and 4 inches long*

· *⅓ cup extra virgin olive oil*

· *2 large cloves garlic, minced*

· *Pinch hot red pepper flakes*

✎ Preheat broiler. Scrub zucchini well (the skin can be gritty) and remove ends. Cut lengthwise into 4 slices about ¼ inch thick.

✎ In a small skillet, heat olive oil, garlic and hot red pepper flakes over moderately low heat until garlic releases its fragrance, about 1 minute. Remove from heat.

✎ Arrange zucchini slices on broiler tray. Brush with olive oil mixture and sprinkle generously with salt. (Do this in batches if your broiler is too small to handle all the zucchini at once.) Broil or grill until lightly browned, then turn, brush with oil again and broil until second side is lightly browned. Remove from heat and transfer zucchini to a cutting board. Slice each

- Salt

- 1 pound dried linguine

- 48 fresh basil leaves, julienned

- 1 cup freshly grated
  pecorino romano cheese

piece lengthwise into 3 or 4 strips. Transfer these to a serving bowl and keep warm in oven preheated to lowest setting.

🖊 Cook pasta in a large pot of boiling salted water until al dente. Transfer with tongs to bowl containing zucchini, allowing a little water to cling to the noodles.

Add basil and any remaining olive oil mixture. Toss well. Add ²⁄₃ cup of the cheese and toss again, adding some of the hot pasta water if necessary to moisten the noodles. Serve immediately on warm dishes. Top each serving with some of the remaining ¹⁄₃ cup cheese. Serves 4.

FUSILLI WITH ZUCCHINI AND TOMATO

YOU CAN USE ALL GREEN ZUCCHINI OR ALL GOLDEN ZUCCHINI, BUT HALF AND HALF MAKES THE PRETTIEST DISH.

- 1 ½ pounds zucchini, preferably some green, some golden

- 1 pound ripe plum tomatoes, peeled and seeded (page 22), then chopped

- 6 tablespoons olive oil

- 4 cloves garlic, minced

- ¼ teaspoon hot
  red pepper flakes

- Salt

- 20 to 30 fresh basil leaves,
  torn into small pieces

- 3 tablespoons capers,
  coarsely chopped

- 1 pound dried fusilli

- 1 cup freshly grated
  pecorino romano cheese

🖊 Scrub zucchini well (the skin can be gritty) and remove ends. Cut lengthwise into slices about ¼ inch thick. Stack the slices and cut crosswise into thin, short sticks. If the zucchini are small — ¾ inch or less in diameter — slice crosswise on the diagonal to make the sticks a little longer.

🖊 In a 12-inch skillet, combine zucchini, tomatoes, 4 tablespoons of the olive oil, garlic, hot red pepper flakes and salt. Cook over moderately high heat, stirring often, until zucchini are tender but not soft and tomatoes have collapsed and formed a thick sauce, about 15 minutes. Toward the end, the mixture will be rather dry and will need to be stirred almost constantly to prevent sticking. Add a few drops of water if necessary.

Remove from heat and stir in basil and capers. Taste and adjust seasoning.

🖊 Cook pasta in a large pot of boiling salted water until al dente. Drain, reserving about ½ cup of the cooking water. Transfer pasta to a large warm bowl. Add the remaining 2 tablespoons oil and toss. Add contents of skillet and cheese and toss again, adding some of the reserved cooking water as needed to thin the sauce. Serve immediately on warm dishes. Serves 4.

LINGUINE WITH GREEN AND GOLDEN ZUCCHINI AND HERB BUTTER

ZUCCHINI DON'T HAVE A LOT OF FLAVOR OF THEIR OWN, WHICH MAKES THEM A NICE FOIL FOR DELICATE SPRING HERBS LIKE TARRAGON, CHIVES AND PARSLEY. FOR A PARTICULARLY ATTRACTIVE DISH, TRY TO FIND BOTH GREEN AND GOLDEN ZUCCHINI AND SOME LAVENDER CHIVE BLOSSOMS TO SPRINKLE ON TOP. THERE'S NO CHEESE IN THIS PASTA, SO BE SURE TO SALT THE SAUCE WELL.

· 1½ pounds zucchini, preferably some green, some golden

· 4 tablespoons unsalted butter

· 2 tablespoons olive oil

· 4 shallots, minced

· Salt and freshly ground black pepper

· 1 teaspoon minced fresh tarragon

· 1 pound fresh linguine

· ⅓ cup chicken stock

· 2 tablespoons minced fresh chives

· ¼ cup minced parsley

· Minced chive blossoms, optional

Scrub zucchini well (the skin can be gritty) and remove ends. Slice ⅛ inch thick on the diagonal, at about a 45° angle. (Discard the chunky first and last pieces.) Stack the slices, two at a time, and cut lengthwise into matchsticks. You should have 1 to 1¼ pounds neatly julienned zucchini.

Melt 2 tablespoons of the butter and the oil in a 12-inch skillet over moderately low heat. Add shallots and sauté until softened, about 2 minutes. Add zucchini. Season highly with salt and pepper. Toss to blend, then raise heat to moderately high and sauté until zucchini are just shy of tender, 3 to 5 minutes. They should still be slightly crisp. Stir in tarragon.

Cook pasta in a large pot of boiling salted water until al dente. While pasta is cooking, add chicken stock to zucchini and reheat briefly. Take care not to overcook the zucchini at this point; they should still have a touch of crispness. Drain pasta. Transfer to a large warm bowl. Add contents of skillet, chives, parsley and the remaining 2 tablespoons butter in small pieces. Toss well. Serve immediately on warm dishes. Top each serving, if desired, with chive blossoms. Serves 4.

PASTA "RISOTTO" WITH BUTTERNUT SQUASH AND LEEKS

THE SLENDER, RICE-SHAPED ROSMARINO PASTA MIMICS THE SHAPE OF A ROSEMARY LEAF. (ORZO IS ABOUT THE SAME SIZE; RISO, ANOTHER SIMILAR PASTA, IS MUCH SHORTER.) IT CAN BE COOKED BY THE SAME METHOD USED FOR RISOTTO, AND THE RESULT WILL BE SURPRISINGLY CLOSE TO THAT CREAMY RICE DISH. IN MY EXPERIENCE WITH THESE PASTA "RISOTTOS" (SEE ALSO PAGES 47 AND 100), HOWEVER, IT DOESN'T MAKE MUCH DIFFERENCE WHETHER YOU ADD THE LIQUID ALL AT ONCE OR A LITTLE AT A TIME. THE IMPORTANT POINT IS TO ADJUST THE HEAT SO THAT THE LIQUID IS ABSORBED BY THE TIME THE PASTA IS COOKED— ABOUT 10 TO 11 MINUTES. IN THIS RECIPE, IT'S ALSO IMPORTANT TO PEEL THE SQUASH THICKLY TO REMOVE ANY TRACES OF HARD SKIN.

- 2 tablespoons unsalted butter

- 1 tablespoon olive oil

- 2 cups thinly sliced leeks, white and pale green parts only

- 3 to 3½ cups diced (⅓ inch) thickly peeled butternut squash (from about 1½ pounds untrimmed squash)

- 1 tablespoon coarsely chopped fresh sage

- Salt and freshly ground black pepper

- Approximately 5 cups hot chicken stock (or part stock/part water)

- 1 pound dried rosmarino or orzo pasta

- 2 tablespoons minced parsley

- ¾ cup freshly grated Parmesan cheese

Heat butter and oil in a 6- to 8-quart heavy-bottomed pot over moderately low heat. Add leeks and sauté until softened, about 5 minutes. Add squash and sage and season with salt and pepper. Add 1 cup of the hot stock and bring to a simmer. Cover and adjust heat to maintain a simmer. Cook until squash is tender, 10 to 15 minutes.

Stir in pasta and 3½ cups of hot stock. Bring to a simmer, adjust heat to maintain a simmer and cook uncovered, stirring frequently, until pasta is al dente and liquid has been absorbed, about 10 minutes. If necessary, add the additional ½ cup hot stock. Whether you need it will depend on the size and shape of your pot and how brisk your heat is. At the end of the cooking time, the mixture should look like a creamy risotto.

Cover, remove from heat and let stand 3 minutes. Uncover and stir in parsley and cheese. Serve immediately in warm bowls. Serves 4.

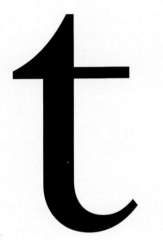

t

TOMATOES

TOMATOES

I COULD EASILY WRITE A SMALL BOOK ON TOMATO SAUCES ALONE, SO RICH AND VARIED IS THIS CATEGORY. IN THE FOLLOWING COLLECTION, YOU WILL FIND MY FAVORITES: RIPE PLUM TOMATOES SIMMERED WITH FENNEL SEED OR WITH ANCHOVIES, A SMOOTH TOMATO SAUCE ENRICHED WITH CREAM, A SPICY TOMATO SAUCE, A ROASTED TOMATO SAUCE, A GREEN TOMATO SAUCE, A DELICATE LASAGNE WITH FRESH TOMATO SAUCE, A WEALTH OF LIGHT SUMMER SAUCES MADE WITH UNCOOKED VINE-RIPENED TOMATOES, AND SEVERAL MORE. ❦ TOMATOES, BOTH FRESH AND CANNED, ARE SO IMPORTANT TO PASTA SAUCERY THAT I HAVE DISCUSSED THEM EXTENSIVELY IN THE INGREDIENTS SECTION (PAGES 21–22). ANY PASTA SAUCE IS ONLY AS GOOD AS ITS INGREDIENTS, BUT THAT TRUTH IS PERHAPS NOWHERE MORE TRUE THAN WITH TOMATO SAUCES. SAVE FRESH TOMATO SAUCES FOR TIMES WHEN YOU CAN FIND TRULY TASTY TOMATOES; AND FOR CANNED TOMATO SAUCES, CHOOSE THE BEST BRAND AVAILABLE.

SPAGHETTI WITH TOMATO AND ANCHOVY SALAD

I COULD HAPPILY EAT THIS PASTA DISH FOR LUNCH TWICE A WEEK IN SUMMER. YOU WILL NEED GREAT-TASTING TOMATOES, OF COURSE; A MIX OF RED AND YELLOW ONES WOULD BE PRETTY. BE SURE TO HAVE SOME BREAD ON HAND FOR SOPPING UP THE DELICIOUS TOMATO JUICES THAT COLLECT ON THE PLATES.

- *1½ pounds ripe tomatoes, peeled and seeded (page 22)*
- *6 tablespoons extra virgin olive oil*
- *8 anchovy fillets, finely minced*
- *2 cloves garlic, minced*
- *⅓ cup minced parsley*
- *2 teaspoons red or white wine vinegar*
- *¼ teaspon hot red pepper flakes*
- *Salt*
- *1 pound dried spaghetti*

❦ Preheat oven to lowest setting.

❦ Slice tomato halves very thinly. If tomatoes are large, cut the halves in half before slicing so slices aren't too long.

❦ In a bowl, combine tomatoes, 4 tablespoons of the olive oil, anchovies, garlic, parsley, wine vinegar, hot red pepper flakes and salt to taste. Stir and set aside.

❦ Place a large serving bowl in the oven with the remaining 2 tablespoons oil and a large pinch of salt.

❦ Cook pasta in a large pot of boiling salted water until al dente. Drain. Transfer to the warmed serving bowl and toss to coat with oil. Place one-quarter of the pasta on each of 4 warm dishes. Top each serving with one-quarter of the tomatoes and their juices and serve immediately. Serves 4.

SPAGHETTI WITH GREEN TOMATOES

GREEN TOMATOES HAVE A PLEASANT ACIDITY THAT MAKES THEM APPEALING IN A PASTA SAUCE. THE BEST TOMATOES FOR THIS DISH ARE ONES THAT HAVE JUST STARTED TO CHANGE COLOR AND SOFTEN. THE FULLY GREEN ONES ARE A LITTLE TOO TART.

IF YOU'RE A GARDENER, YOU KNOW WHERE TO FIND PLENTY OF GREEN TOMATOES. IF YOU'RE NOT, CHECK FARMERS' MARKETS IN SUMMER OR ASK PRODUCE MERCHANTS IF THEY CAN GET THEM FOR YOU. FULLY GREEN TOMATOES WILL BEGIN TO DEVELOP A PRETTY BLUSH AFTER A FEW DAYS AT ROOM TEMPERATURE.

· 2 pounds green tomatoes with some pink blush

· ¼ cup extra virgin olive oil

· 4 cloves garlic, minced

· ¼ teaspoon hot red pepper flakes

· Salt

· 1 pound dried spaghetti

· Approximately 24 fresh basil leaves

· 1 cup freshly grated pecorino romano cheese

🖉 Core tomatoes and cut them in half through the stem end. Cut each half into thin wedges. Set aside.

🖉 Heat olive oil in a 12-inch skillet over moderately low heat. Add garlic and sauté 1 minute to release its fragrance. Add tomatoes, hot red pepper flakes and salt to taste. Cover, adjust heat to maintain a simmer and cook until tomatoes soften and lose their shape and begin to settle into a coarse sauce, about 15 minutes. Taste and adjust seasoning.

🖉 Cook pasta in a large pot of boiling salted water until al dente. Tear basil leaves into small pieces. Transfer pasta with tongs to a large warm bowl, allowing a little water to cling to the pasta. Add sauce and basil and toss. Add cheese and toss again. Serve immediately on warm dishes. Serves 4.

SPAGHETTI WITH SICILIAN TOMATO AND ALMOND SAUCE

THE SICILIAN TOWN OF TRAPANI IS THE SOURCE OF THIS SAUCE, A COARSE PESTO MADE WITH TOMATO AND ALMONDS. TOASTING THE ALMONDS ISN'T TRADITIONAL, BUT I THINK IT IMPROVES THE FLAVOR. THE NUTTY AROMA RELEASED WHEN YOU TOSS THIS PESTO WITH HOT PASTA WILL MAKE YOUR MOUTH WATER.

· ⅔ cup blanched almonds

· 1 pound ripe plum tomatoes, peeled and seeded (page 22)

· 2 cloves garlic, thinly sliced

· 1 cup lightly packed fresh basil leaves

🖉 Preheat oven to 350°F. Spread almonds on a baking sheet or in a pie pan and toast until lightly browned, about 15 minutes. Let cool.

🖉 In a food processor, combine almonds, tomatoes, garlic, basil and hot red pepper flakes. Process until well chopped, stopping once or twice to scrape down the

Tomatoes

- Pinch hot red pepper flakes
- ⅓ cup extra virgin olive oil
- Salt
- 1 pound dried spaghetti

sides of the bowl. With motor running, add oil through the feed tube until mixture is well blended but not completely smooth; a little texture is nice in this sauce. Transfer to a bowl and add salt to taste.

❂ Cook pasta in a large pot of boiling salted water until al dente. Transfer with tongs to a large warm bowl, allowing a little water to cling to the noodles. Add sauce and toss, adding a little of the cooking water if necessary to help the sauce coat the noodles nicely. Serve immediately on warm dishes. Serves 4.

PERCIATELLI WITH TOMATO-FENNEL SAUCE

SOMETIMES THE ADDITION OF A SINGLE HERB OR SPICE CAN MAKE A FAMILIAR DISH TASTE ENTIRELY NEW. I LOVE A PINCH OF FENNEL SEED IN A BASIC TOMATO SAUCE, FOR EXAMPLE; THE SWEET LICORICE-LIKE AROMA ADDS AN APPEALING DIMENSION TO THE DISH.

FOR BEST RESULTS, START WITH WHOLE FENNEL SEED AND GRIND IT IN A MORTAR AND PESTLE OR A SPICE GRINDER. IT DOESN'T HAVE TO BE GROUND TO A POWDER, BUT IT SHOULD BE FINE ENOUGH THAT YOU DON'T TASTE TOUGH LITTLE BITS OF FENNEL SEED IN THE SAUCE.

- ⅓ cup olive oil
- 2 large cloves garlic, minced
- 1½ pounds ripe plum tomatoes, diced
- ¼ teaspoon hot red pepper flakes
- 1 teaspoon freshly ground fennel seed
- Salt
- 1 pound dried perciatelli, bucatini or penne rigate (ridged tubes)
- 1 cup freshly grated pecorino romano cheese

❂ Heat olive oil in a 12-inch skillet over moderately low heat. Add garlic and sauté 1 minute to release its fragrance. Add tomatoes, hot red pepper flakes, fennel seed and salt to taste. Raise heat to moderately high and cook, stirring often, until tomatoes are reduced to a thick and nearly smooth sauce, 15 to 20 minutes. Add a little water as needed to keep sauce from sticking; cover skillet if needed during the last few minutes to help tomatoes soften.

❂ Cook pasta in a large pot of boiling salted water until al dente. Transfer with tongs to a large warm bowl, allowing a little water to cling to the noodles. Add contents of skillet and toss to coat. Add all but 2 tablespoons of the cheese and toss again, adding a little of the cooking water as needed to thin the sauce. Serve immediately on warm dishes, topping each serving with some of the remaining 2 tablespoons cheese. Serves 4.

SUMMER LASAGNE WITH FRESH TOMATO AND CHEESE

AS LASAGNE GOES, THIS ONE IS EASY BECAUSE IT DOESN'T CALL FOR BÉCHAMEL SAUCE. NEVERTHELESS, I FIND THAT IT TAKES ABOUT 90 MINUTES TO ASSEMBLE—OR AN HOUR IF I CAN ENLIST SOME HELP. THE REWARD IS A PARTICULARLY DELICATE AND AROMATIC LASAGNE, WITH VERY THIN LAYERS OF PASTA AND CREAMY FILLING.

IF YOU BUY FRESH PASTA SHEETS, YOU'LL PROBABLY NEED TO ROLL THEM THINNER AT HOME—THROUGH THE NUMBER 5 SETTING ON THE ATLAS PASTA MACHINE. YOU NEED ¾ POUND OF PASTA FOR THIS DISH, BUT I RECOMMEND HAVING 1 POUND ON HAND IN CASE SOME SHEETS TEAR AS YOU COOK THEM. IF YOU MAKE YOUR OWN PASTA, ROLL IT OUT AS DIRECTED ON PAGE 24, LEAVING THE SHEETS AS WIDE AS THEY COME FROM THE PASTA MACHINE.

· 6 tablespoons olive oil

· 4 cloves garlic, minced

· 2½ pounds ripe plum tomatoes, peeled and seeded (page 22), then chopped

· 2 tablespoons minced fresh basil

· 1 teaspoon minced fresh marjoram

· Salt and freshly ground black pepper

· ¾ pound whole-milk ricotta cheese (about 1½ cups)

· 2½ tablespoons unsalted butter, softened

· ¾ cup freshly grated Parmesan cheese

· ¼ cup minced parsley

· ¾ to 1 pound fresh egg or spinach pasta, in wide sheets

· ½ pound whole-milk mozzarella cheese, grated

Heat 5 tablespoons of the olive oil in a 12-inch skillet over moderately low heat. Add garlic and sauté 1 minute to release its fragrance. Add tomatoes, cover and adjust heat to maintain a simmer. Cook until tomatoes have softened and collapsed into a near-purée, about 15 minutes. Uncover and add basil, marjoram and salt and pepper to taste. Simmer, stirring occasionally, until tomatoes have cooked down into a thick, nearly smooth sauce. Taste and adjust seasoning. You should have about 2 cups.

Put ricotta, 2 tablespoons of the butter and salt and pepper to taste in a food processor and process until smooth. Transfer to a bowl and stir in ¼ cup of the Parmesan and all the parsley.

Bring a large pot of salted water to a boil. Fill a large bowl three-fourths full with ice water and stir in the remaining 1 tablespoon olive oil. If you are using store-bought fresh pasta, it is probably not thin enough. Cut the sheets into manageable widths and roll them through your own pasta machine to make them thinner (see introduction).

Boil the sheets, two at a time, for 15 seconds. Carefully transfer to ice water and stir to make sure they do not stick to each other or themselves.

Preheat oven to 400°F. Using remaining ½ tablespoon butter, butter the bottom and sides of a 9-by-13-inch baking dish. →

To assemble lasagne lift sheets of pasta out of the ice water, as you need them, and pat them thoroughly dry between two dish towels. Line the bottom of the baking dish with pasta cut to fit, with no overlap. Spread one-sixth of the tomato sauce evenly over the noodles. Top with one-third of the mozzarella. Top mozzarella with a second layer of pasta, cut to fit. Spread another one-sixth of the sauce evenly over the noodles. Top with half the whipped ricotta. You won't be able to spread it evenly, but you can spoon it on in small neat clumps. Repeat with pasta, sauce, mozzarella; pasta, sauce, ricotta; pasta, sauce, mozzarella; pasta, sauce and remaining ½ cup Parmesan.

Bake until cheese on top has melted and is beginning to brown and lasagne is hot throughout, about 20 minutes. Let stand 15 minutes before cutting. Serve on warm dishes. Serves 6.

SPAGHETTI WITH MARINATED TOMATOES AND GOAT CHEESE

· *1 ½ pounds ripe tomatoes, peeled and seeded (page 22)*

· *5 tablespoons extra virgin olive oil*

· *2 cloves garlic, very finely minced*

· *¼ teaspoon hot red pepper flakes*

· *3 tablespoons minced capers*

· *Salt*

· *1 pound dried spaghetti*

· *30 to 40 fresh basil leaves*

· *¼ pound goat cheese, cut into olive-sized pieces (see introduction)*

IN LATE SUMMER, WHEN THE LOCAL TOMATOES ARE RIPE, IT SEEMS THAT I CAN NEVER HAVE TOO MANY RECIPES FOR DISHES LIKE THIS ONE—A VARIATION ON THE HOT PASTA—COLD TOMATO THEME. THE LITTLE NUGGETS OF GOAT CHEESE STIRRED INTO THE TOMATOES JUST BEFORE YOU ADD THE PASTA MELT DOWN TO MAKE A DELICIOUS SAUCE. I TYPICALLY USE MONTRACHET FROM FRANCE, BUT ANY GOAT CHEESE THAT IS FIRM YET CREAMY WILL DO. FOR AN EVEN PRETTIER DISH, TRY A MIX OF RED AND YELLOW TOMATOES.

Slice tomato halves very thinly. If tomatoes are large, cut the halves in half before slicing so slices aren't too long.

Transfer tomatoes to a serving bowl and add olive oil, garlic, hot red pepper flakes, capers and salt to taste. Stir to blend.

Cook pasta in a large pot of boiling salted water until al dente. Just before pasta is ready, tear basil leaves into small pieces. Stir basil and goat cheese into tomato mixture. Drain pasta, add to bowl containing the tomato mixture and toss. Serve immediately on warm dishes. Serves 4.

PENNE WITH WINTER TOMATO SAUCE

TO MAKE A TASTY TOMATO SAUCE IN WINTER, YOU NEED GOOD CANNED TOMATOES. SAMPLE THE BRANDS AVAILABLE IN YOUR AREA TO FIND THE ONE YOU LIKE BEST. CONTRARY TO POPULAR BELIEF, IMPORTED ITALIAN CANNED TOMATOES AREN'T ALWAYS SUPERIOR. I PARTICULARLY LIKE A DOMESTIC PACKER CALLED MUIR GLEN. THE TOMATOES ARE ORGANICALLY GROWN AND THEY HAVE A RICH, SWEET FLAVOR.

THE OTHER KEY TO SUCCESS WITH THIS SAUCE IS TO COOK THE VEGETABLES UNTIL THEIR NATURAL SUGARS BEGIN TO CARAMELIZE BEFORE YOU ADD THE TOMATOES. THESE LIGHTLY CARAMELIZED VEGETABLES WILL SWEETEN YOUR SAUCE.

- *⅓ cup olive oil*
- *1 medium yellow onion, minced*
- *2 celery ribs, cut into small neat dice*
- *1 large or 2 small carrots, peeled and cut into small neat dice*
- *2 large cloves garlic, minced*
- *2½ cups strained canned tomatoes (pages 21–22)*
- *1 bay leaf*
- *¼ teaspoon hot red pepper flakes*
- *Salt*
- *Approximately ½ teaspoon sugar, optional*
- *1 pound dried penne rigate (ridged tubes)*
- *2 tablespoons minced parsley*
- *Freshly grated Parmesan cheese for passing*

Heat olive oil in a 12-inch skillet over moderate heat. Add onion, celery and carrot and sauté, stirring often, until vegetables soften and begin to color, 15 to 20 minutes. Add garlic and sauté until fragrant, about 1 minute. Add tomatoes to skillet along with bay leaf, hot red pepper flakes and a large pinch of salt. If tomatoes taste more tart than sweet, add a little sugar. Bring mixture to a simmer, then adjust heat to maintain a simmer and cook, stirring often, until mixture is thick and tasty, about 30 minutes. If the mixture gets too thick before the flavors have melded and vegetables have softened, add a little water and continue cooking. When the taste and texture are to your liking, remove bay leaf.

Cook pasta in a large pot of boiling salted water until al dente. Drain, reserving about ½ cup of the cooking water. Transfer pasta to a large warm bowl. Add sauce and toss, adding hot water if necessary to help the sauce coat the noodles nicely. Serve immediately on warm dishes, topping each serving with parsley. Pass the Parmesan at the table. Serves 4.

Tomatoes

BAKED RIGATONI WITH TOMATO SAUCE AND MOZZARELLA

WATCH YOUR TABLECLOTH WHEN YOU SERVE THIS DISH. THE MELTED MOZZARELLA MAKES
LONG, THREADLIKE STRINGS WHEN YOU LIFT UP A SPOONFUL OF NOODLES. THE DISH
NEEDS TO BE SERVED IMMEDIATELY AND EATEN WITHOUT DELAY, WHILE THE MOZZARELLA
IS STILL MOLTEN.

- *3 tablespoons olive oil*

- *2 large cloves garlic, minced*

- *2 cups strained canned tomatoes (pages 21–22)*

- *½ tablespoon minced fresh oregano*

- *1 tablespoon minced parsley*

- *¼ teaspoon hot red pepper flakes, or to taste*

- *Salt*

- *1 pound dried rigatoni*

- *4 ounces whole-milk mozzarella cheese, thinly sliced*

- *⅓ cup freshly grated Parmesan cheese*

❦ Preheat oven to 375°F. Heat olive oil in a 10-inch skillet over moderately low heat. Add garlic and sauté 1 minute to release its fragrance. Add tomatoes, oregano, parsley, hot red pepper flakes and salt to taste. Bring to a simmer, adjust heat to maintain a simmer and cook until sauce is thick and tasty, 20 to 25 minutes.

❦ Cook pasta in a large pot of boiling salted water until about two-thirds done, about 8 minutes. Drain and return to pot. Set aside ⅓ cup sauce and add rest to pasta. Toss to coat. Put one-third of the pasta in a baking dish with a 10- to 12-cup capacity. Top with half the mozzarella cheese. Add half of the remaining pasta, then the remaining mozzarella cheese.

Top with the remaining pasta. Drizzle with the reserved ⅓ cup sauce. Sprinkle Parmesan evenly over the top. Cover and bake until bubbling hot, about 15 minutes. Serve immediately on warm plates. Serves 4.

RIGATONI WITH SUMMER TOMATO SAUCE

I PUT UP PINT AFTER PINT OF THIS SAUCE IN THE SUMMER AS MY HOMEGROWN PLUM TOMATOES RIPEN. WHEN YOU HAVE RIPE TOMATOES IN YOUR GARDEN OR CAN FIND THEM AT THE MARKET, TAKE TIME TO MAKE SEVERAL BATCHES OF THIS SAUCE. THE RECIPE DOUBLES WELL AND THE SAUCE FREEZES BEAUTIFULLY. YOU WILL PAT YOURSELF ON THE BACK IN THE MIDDLE OF WINTER WHEN YOU OPEN A FREEZER CONTAINER AND FIND THE SWEET TASTE OF VINE-RIPENED TOMATOES INSIDE. I THANK COOKBOOK AUTHOR MARCELLA HAZAN, WHOSE TOMATO SAUCE RECIPE INSPIRED THIS ONE.

IF YOU WOULD LIKE TO CAN THIS SAUCE, PLEASE CALL OR WRITE YOUR COUNTY AGRICULTURAL EXTENSION OFFICE AND ASK FOR THE LATEST GUIDELINES ON CANNING TOMATO PRODUCTS. DEPENDING ON THE ACIDITY OF YOUR TOMATOES, YOU MAY NEED TO ADD LEMON JUICE OR VINEGAR TO THE SAUCE TO MAKE IT SAFE TO CAN BY THE WATER-BATH METHOD.

For the Summer Tomato Sauce:

· *2 pounds ripe plum tomatoes, quartered*

· *¼ cup extra virgin olive oil*

· *⅓ cup minced carrot*

· *⅓ cup minced celery*

· *⅓ cup minced yellow onion*

· *1 large clove garlic, minced*

· *½ tablespoon minced fresh oregano*

· *1 tablespoon minced parsley*

· *Salt*

· *Pinch hot red pepper flakes, optional*

· *Pinch sugar, optional*

· *1 pound rigatoni, penne rigate (ridged tubes) or other short pasta*

· *½ cup freshly grated Parmesan cheese, plus additional Parmesan cheese for passing*

To make sauce, put quartered tomatoes in a heavy, medium saucepan. Cover and simmer over moderate heat until tomatoes have collapsed and rendered their juices, about 15 minutes, uncovering and stirring once or twice to make sure they are not sticking to the pan bottom. Uncover, adjust heat to maintain a slow simmer and cook, stirring occasionally, until tomatoes have reduced to a thick, saucelike consistency, about 45 minutes. Pass the tomatoes through a food mill placed over a bowl to remove skins and seeds. You should have about 2 cups purée.

Heat olive oil in a 10-inch skillet over moderately low heat. Add carrot, celery, onion, garlic, oregano and parsley. Cook, stirring occasionally, until vegetables are soft and sweet, about 30 minutes. Add tomato purée. Stir to blend. Season with salt and, if desired, hot red pepper flakes and sugar if the tomatoes seem too tart. Cover and simmer over low heat for 10 minutes to blend flavors. Taste and adjust seasoning. You should have about 2 cups sauce.

Cook pasta in a large pot of boiling salted water until al dente. Drain, reserving about ½ cup of the cooking water. Transfer pasta to a warm bowl. Add sauce and toss to coat. Add ½ cup Parmesan cheese and toss again, adding some of the reserved cooking water if needed to thin the sauce. Serve immediately on warm dishes and pass additional cheese at the table. Serves 4.

PERCIATELLI WITH SPICY TOMATO SAUCE

THIS IRRESISTIBLE TOMATO SAUCE WOULD TASTE GOOD ON ALMOST ANY DRIED PASTA SHAPE, BUT I PARTICULARLY LIKE IT ON PERCIATELLI (ALSO KNOWN AS BUCATINI), THE HOLLOW STRANDS THAT LOOK LIKE THICK SPAGHETTI.

· 2 tablespoons olive oil

· 3 to 4 ounces pancetta, minced

· 2 large cloves garlic, minced

· Scant ¼ teaspoon
hot red pepper flakes

· 1½ pounds ripe
plum tomatoes, diced

· Salt

· 1 pound dried perciatelli
or bucatini

· Approximately ¾ cup
freshly grated ricotta salata,
aged goat or pecorino
romano cheese

· 2 tablespoons minced parsley

❦ Put olive oil and pancetta in a 12-inch skillet. Cook over moderate heat, stirring occasionally, until pancetta begins to crisp, 3 to 5 minutes. Add garlic and sauté 1 minute to release its fragrance. Add hot red pepper flakes, tomatoes and a generous pinch of salt. Raise heat to moderately high and simmer, stirring often, until tomatoes collapse and form a thick sauce, 15 to 20 minutes. Add as much water as necessary to keep mixture from sticking, and cover skillet during the last few minutes if necessary to help tomatoes soften.

❦ Cook pasta in a large pot of boiling salted water until al dente. Transfer with tongs to a large warm bowl, allowing a little water to cling to the noodles. Add sauce and toss to coat, adding a little pasta cooking water if needed to thin the sauce. Serve on warm dishes, topping each serving with some of the grated cheese and parsley. Serves 4.

PAPPARDELLE WITH CREAMY TOMATO SAUCE

IT'S SURPRISING HOW LITTLE CREAM IT TAKES TO MAKE A TOMATO SAUCE RICH AND MELLOW. THE CREAM GIVES THIS SAUCE A MORE VELVETY TEXTURE, TOO, WHICH IS PARTICULARLY APPEALING WITH THE WIDE PAPPARDELLE.

· ¼ cup olive oil

· 2 large cloves garlic, minced

· 1½ pounds ripe plum tomatoes, peeled and seeded (page 22), then chopped

· Salt and freshly ground black pepper

· ¼ cup heavy cream

· Pinch sugar, optional

· 1 pound fresh pappardelle (about ½ inch wide)

· ⅔ cup freshly grated Parmesan cheese, plus additional Parmesan cheese for passing if desired

· 2 tablespoons minced parsley

✐ Heat olive oil in a 12-inch skillet over moderately low heat. Add garlic and sauté 1 minute to release its fragrance. Add tomatoes and salt and pepper to taste. Cover and adjust heat to maintain a simmer. Cook until tomatoes are quite soft and have collapsed into a near-purée, about 10 minutes. Uncover and cook, stirring often, until mixture is very smooth, about 10 minutes. Add water as necessary to keep sauce from sticking. Stir in cream. Taste and add sugar if sauce seems a bit tart. Simmer briefly to incorporate the cream, adding enough water to bring sauce to desired consistency. Taste and adjust seasoning.

✐ Cook pasta in a large pot of boiling salted water until al dente. Drain, reserving about ½ cup of the cooking water. Transfer pasta to a large warm bowl. Add sauce, ⅔ cup Parmesan cheese and 1 tablespoon of the parsley. Toss, adding a little of the reserved cooking water if necessary to thin the sauce. Serve immediately on warm dishes, topping each serving with some of the remaining 1 tablespoon parsley. Pass additional cheese at the table, if desired. Serves 4.

PENNE WITH TOMATO AND OLIVE SAUCE

HERE'S A LIVELY, EASY TOMATO SAUCE THAT TAKES LESS THAN 30 MINUTES TO MAKE. I LOVE ITS PUNGENT, PEPPERY TASTE AND THE ROUGH TEXTURE OF CHOPPED OLIVES AND CAPERS. MY PREFERENCE HERE IS FOR PICHOLINE OLIVES, WHICH AREN'T DIFFICULT TO PIT BY HAND. USE THE BEST-TASTING OLIVES AVAILABLE TO YOU; EVEN A BLACK OLIVE, SUCH AS A GREEK KALAMATA, WOULD BE ALL RIGHT.

· ¼ cup olive oil

· 2 large cloves garlic, minced

· ¼ teaspoon hot
red pepper flakes

· 2 cups strained canned
tomatoes (pages 21–22)

· 5 or 6 anchovy fillets,
finely minced

· 1 cup coarsely chopped,
pitted green olives, preferably
picholine

· 2 tablespoons capers,
rinsed and coarsely chopped

· 3 tablespoons minced parsley

· Salt

· 1 pound dried penne rigate
(ridged tubes)

❦ Heat olive oil in a 10- or 12-inch skillet over moderately low heat. Add garlic and sauté 1 minute to release its fragrance. Add hot red pepper flakes and tomatoes and bring to a simmer. Adjust heat to maintain a simmer and cook, stirring often, until sauce is quite thick, about 20 minutes. Add anchovies, olives, capers, 2 tablespoons of the parsley and salt to taste. Remove from heat; reheat sauce gently just before you are ready to toss it with the pasta.

❦ Cook pasta in a large pot of boiling salted water until al dente. Drain. Transfer to a large warm bowl. Add sauce and toss. Serve immediately on warm dishes, topping each serving with some of the remaining 1 tablespoon parsley. Serves 4.

GNOCCHETTI RIGATI WITH TOMATO-PORCINI SAUCE

THIS SAUCE DEVELOPS ITS FLAVOR THROUGH A TWO-PART PROCESS: FIRST, A SLOW SAUTÉING OF THE AROMATIC VEGETABLES UNTIL THEY BEGIN TO CARAMELIZE; THEN, A SLOW SIMMERING OF THE SAUCE TO REDUCE IT, EXTRACT THE FLAVOR OF VEGETABLES AND MUSHROOMS AND BLEND THE ELEMENTS. INTERESTINGLY, THE SAUCE IS EVEN BETTER THE NEXT DAY.

ROSEMARY CAN VARY A LOT IN STRENGTH. START WITH 1/2 TEASPOON, THEN ADD MORE IF YOU THINK THE SAUCE NEEDS IT.

- *½ ounce dried porcini*
- *¼ cup olive oil*
- *½ cup minced yellow onion*
- *½ cup minced carrot*
- *3 or 4 large cloves garlic, minced*
- *½ teaspoon minced fresh rosemary, or more to taste*
- *3 cups strained canned tomatoes (pages 21–22)*
- *½ cup chicken stock*
- *Salt and freshly ground black pepper*
- *Pinch sugar, optional*
- *1 pound dried gnocchetti rigati (large ridged tubes), penne rigate (ridged tubes) or rigatoni*
- *¾ cup freshly grated Parmesan cheese*

❧ Put porcini in a small bowl with 1 cup warm water and let stand 1 hour to soften. Lift porcini out with a slotted spoon and chop medium-fine. Strain soaking liquid through a sieve lined with dampened cheesecloth and save to thin sauce or for another use, such as a soup or stew.

❧ Heat olive oil in a 12-inch skillet over moderately low heat. Add onion, carrot, garlic and ½ teaspoon rosemary and sauté until vegetables are soft and sweet, about 20 minutes. Add tomatoes, chopped porcini and chicken stock. Season with salt and pepper and add sugar if tomatoes seem too tart. Bring to a simmer, adjust heat to maintain a simmer and cook, uncovered, until sauce is thick and tasty, about 40 minutes. The lengthy cooking time helps to develop flavor. If sauce threatens to stick, add a tablespoon or two of water or strained porcini soaking liquid. At the end of the cooking time, taste and adjust seasoning. Keep warm.

❧ Cook pasta in a large pot of boiling salted water until al dente. Drain, reserving about ½ cup of the cooking water. Transfer pasta to a large warm bowl. Add contents of skillet and toss. Add cheese and toss again, adding some of the reserved cooking water if needed to thin the sauce. Serve immediately on warm dishes. Serves 4.

CONCHIGLIE RIGATE WITH TOMATOES AND CHICK-PEAS

SOMEHOW THE CHICK-PEAS ALWAYS FIND THEIR WAY INTO THE COZY HOLLOWS OF THE PASTA SHELLS.

· 6 tablespoons olive oil

· 4 cloves garlic, minced

· 1½ pounds ripe plum tomatoes, diced

· ¼ teaspoon hot red pepper flakes

· Salt

· 2 cups drained cooked chick-peas (drained and rinsed, if canned)

· 1 pound dried conchiglie rigate ("ridged shells")

· ¼ cup minced parsley

· ½ cup coarsely chopped fresh basil

· 1 cup freshly grated pecorino romano cheese

❦ Heat olive oil in a 12-inch skillet over moderately low heat. Add garlic and sauté 1 minute to release its fragrance. Add tomatoes, hot red pepper flakes and salt to taste. Raise heat to moderately high and sauté, stirring often, until tomatoes collapse and form a thick sauce, 15 to 20 minutes. Add a little water if necessary to keep sauce from sticking, and cover skillet if needed during the last few minutes to help tomatoes soften. Stir in chick-peas. Taste and adjust seasoning.

❦ Cook pasta in a large pot of boiling salted water until al dente. Drain, reserving about ½ cup of the cooking water. Transfer pasta to a large warm bowl. Add sauce, parsley and basil and toss. Add cheese and toss again, adding some of the reserved cooking water as necessary to help the sauce coat the noodles nicely. Serve immediately on warm dishes. Serves 4.

RIGATONI WITH ROASTED TOMATO AND GARLIC SAUCE

SLOW OVEN ROASTING TURNS TOMATOES AND GARLIC SWEET AND MELLOW. ROAST THEM TOGETHER WITH HERBS AND OIL, THEN PASS THROUGH A FOOD MILL TO MAKE AN EASY, FLAVOR-PACKED SAUCE.

- ¼ cup plus 2 tablespoons extra virgin olive oil
- 8 fresh thyme sprigs
- 12 large cloves garlic, unpeeled
- 1½ pounds ripe plum tomatoes, halved
- Salt and freshly ground black pepper
- 1 pound dried rigatoni
- ¾ cup freshly grated ricotta salata or pecorino romano cheese

❧ Preheat oven to 300°F. Put ¼ cup oil, thyme sprigs and garlic cloves in a baking dish and roll the garlic around to coat with oil. Add tomatoes to the dish, cut side down.

❧ Bake 30 minutes, then test a clove of garlic for doneness: it is done when the flesh inside the papery skin is just soft enough to mash to a paste. Remove the garlic as soon as it is done; continue baking tomatoes. After 1 hour, turn tomatoes cut side up, season generously with salt and pepper and spoon some of the pan juices over them. Continue baking tomatoes until they are quite soft, another 45 to 60 minutes. Discard thyme sprigs.

❧ Slip a few of the soft garlic cloves out of their skin and pass them and the tomatoes through a food mill placed over a 12-inch skillet. I find that 6 to 8 cloves is usually enough to give an appealing roasted garlic flavor; add more of the baked cloves if you like. (Any leftover cloves can be spread on toast for the chef.) Stir any oil or juices in the bottom of the baking dish into the purée.

❧ Add remaining 2 tablespoons oil and reheat gently over low heat. Taste and adjust seasoning.

❧ Cook pasta in a large pot of boiling salted water until al dente. Drain, reserving about ½ cup of the cooking water. Transfer pasta to a large warm bowl. Add sauce and toss to coat. Add ½ cup of the cheese and toss again, adding some of the reserved cooking water if needed to thin the sauce. Serve immediately on warm dishes, topping each serving with some of the remaining ¼ cup cheese. Serves 4.

SPAGHETTI WITH TOMATOES, GREEK OLIVES AND FETA

THIS IS A DISH FOR A WARM SUMMER NIGHT, WHEN THE IDEA OF PASTA WITH AN UNCOOKED SAUCE APPEALS.

· 1 ½ pounds ripe tomatoes, peeled and seeded (page 22)

· 24 black olives, preferably Kalamata, pitted and coarsely chopped

· 2 tablespoons capers, rinsed and coarsely chopped

· 2 cloves garlic, finely minced

· ¼ teaspoon hot red pepper flakes

· ¼ cup extra virgin olive oil

· 2 teaspoons white wine vinegar

· Salt

· 1 pound dried spaghetti

· Approximately 40 small fresh basil leaves

· 6 ounces Greek or Bulgarian feta cheese

Slice tomato halves very thinly. If tomatoes are large, cut the halves in half before slicing so slices aren't too long.

In a large bowl, combine tomatoes, olives, capers, garlic, hot red pepper flakes, olive oil, wine vinegar and a generous pinch of salt. Stir gently to blend.

Cook pasta in a large pot of boiling salted water until al dente. Just before pasta is ready, tear basil leaves into small pieces, add to tomato mixture and stir.

Drain pasta and add to bowl. Toss well. Grate the feta directly into the bowl and toss again so that feta melts and forms a creamy sauce. Serve immediately on warm dishes. Serves 4.

RIGATONI WITH NEAPOLITAN TOMATO SAUCE

THIS THICK, SMOOTH, HERBED PURÉE IS A BASIC SOUTHERN ITALIAN TOMATO SAUCE. UNLIKE SUMMER TOMATO SAUCE (PAGE 140), THIS SAUCE IS MADE WITH CANNED TOMATOES; SAUTÉED AROMATIC VEGETABLES SIMMERED AND PURÉED WITH THE TOMATOES ADD TEXTURE AND SWEETNESS. IF YOU PREFER, SUBSTITUTE FRESH BASIL OR A LITTLE ROSEMARY FOR THE OREGANO OR MARJORAM. AND WHEN TOMATOES ARE IN SEASON, YOU CAN—INDEED SHOULD—MAKE THE SAUCE WITH FRESH TOMATOES.

For the Neapolitan Tomato Sauce:

· *3 tablespoons extra virgin olive oil*

· *½ small yellow onion, diced*

· *1 small carrot, diced*

· *1 celery rib, diced*

· *2 large cloves garlic, minced*

· *1 tablespoon minced parsley*

· *2 teaspoons minced fresh oregano or marjoram*

· *2 cups canned plum tomatoes, with juice*

· *Salt and freshly ground black pepper*

· *Pinch sugar, optional*

· *1 pound dried rigatoni*

· *½ cup freshly grated Parmesan, plus additional Parmesan cheese for passing*

To make sauce, heat 2 tablespoons of the olive oil in a 10-inch skillet over moderately low heat. Add onion, carrot, celery, garlic, parsley and oregano. Sauté until vegetables are soft and sweet, about 15 minutes. Stir in tomatoes, crushing them between your fingers as you add them. Season with salt and pepper. Bring to a simmer, then cover and adjust heat to maintain a simmer. Cook 45 minutes. Pass sauce through a food mill placed over a clean skillet, making sure you get as much of the vegetables through the mill as possible. Add the remaining tablespoon oil and reheat gently. Taste and adjust seasoning, adding sugar if sauce seems a little tart. Keep warm.

Cook pasta in a large pot of boiling salted water until al dente. Drain. Transfer to a large warm bowl. Add sauce and toss. Serve immediately on warm dishes, topping each serving with some of the ½ cup Parmesan cheese. Pass additional cheese at the table. Serves 4.

V

MIXED VEGETABLE SAUCES

MIXED VEGETABLE SAUCES

VEGETABLES IN COMBINATION MAKE SOME OF THE MOST PLEASING PASTA SAUCES. IN THE FOLLOWING COLLECTION, YOU'LL FIND SAUCES WHERE NO ONE VEGETABLE DOMINATES. INSTEAD, TWO OR MORE COMPLEMENTARY VEGETABLES BLEND HARMONIOUSLY.

LINGUINE WITH LEEKS, PEAS, SAFFRON AND CREAM

IT'S NOT EASY TO GIVE A PRECISE MEASUREMENT FOR SAFFRON THREADS. PACK THEM LOOSELY IN THE MEASURING SPOON; YOU DON'T NEED MUCH. SAFFRON IS A SEDUCTIVE BUT POWERFUL FLAVOR; BETTER TO USE TOO LITTLE THAN TOO MUCH.

- 5 tablespoons unsalted butter
- 2 cups thinly sliced leeks, white and pale green parts only
- 1½ cups freshly shelled English peas (about 1½ pounds unshelled) or frozen petite peas
- 1 cup chicken stock
- ¼ teaspoon loosely packed saffron threads (about 30 threads)
- ½ cup heavy cream
- Salt and freshly ground black pepper
- ¼ cup minced parsley
- 1 pound fresh linguine

Melt 4 tablespoons of the butter in a 12-inch skillet over moderate heat. Add leeks and sauté until softened, about 5 minutes. Add peas, stock and saffron. Bring to a simmer, cover and adjust heat to maintain a bare simmer. Cook until peas are just tender, 6 to 8 minutes for fresh peas and 4 to 5 minutes for frozen peas. Uncover, add cream and simmer briefly until cream has reduced and thickened slightly. Don't let it reduce too much; fresh pasta soaks up a lot of sauce. Season with salt and pepper. Stir in parsley.

Cook pasta in a large pot of boiling salted water until al dente. Drain, reserving about ½ cup of the pasta cooking water. Transfer pasta to a large warm bowl. Add remaining 1 tablespoon butter and the sauce and toss to coat, thinning the sauce if necessary with a little of the reserved cooking water. Serve immediately on warm dishes. Serves 4.

ORECCHIETTE WITH ARTICHOKES, PEAS AND FAVA BEANS

IN SPRING, WHEN ARTICHOKES, PEAS AND FAVA BEANS APPEAR IN THE MARKET AT THE SAME TIME, YOU CAN BRAISE THEM TOGETHER TO MAKE A SAUCE FOR ORECCHIETTE. SHELLING ALL THOSE PEAS AND BEANS CAN BE TEDIOUS BY YOURSELF, HOWEVER; SAVE THIS DISH FOR AN EVENING WHEN YOU HAVE KITCHEN HELPERS.

154

- *3 pounds fresh fava beans*
- *12 baby artichokes, 1½ to 2 ounces each*
- *½ lemon*
- *3 tablespoons unsalted butter*
- *2 tablespoons olive oil*
- *Salt and freshly ground black pepper*
- *1½ cups freshly shelled English peas (about 2 pounds unshelled)*
- *1 cup thinly sliced green onions (scallions), white and pale green parts only*
- *1 pound dried orecchiette ("little ears")*
- *1 cup freshly grated Parmesan cheese*

Remove fava beans from their fuzzy pods. To peel the individual beans, blanch them in boiling water about 30 seconds if they are small, up to a minute if they are large. Drain. While they are hot, pinch open the end of the bean opposite the end that connected it to the pod. The peeled bean will slip out easily.

Peel back the outer leaves on each artichoke until they break off at the base. Keep removing leaves until you reach the pale green heart. Cut about ⅓ inch off the top of the heart to remove the pointed tips; cut away any stem. Trim the base to remove any dark green parts. Cut each heart in half lengthwise, then quarter each half lengthwise. Drop artichokes as they are cut into a bowl of water acidulated with the juice of the lemon half.

Melt 2 tablespoons of the butter with the oil in a 12-inch skillet over moderate heat. Drain artichokes and add to skillet. Season to taste with salt and pepper, cover and cook 5 minutes. Add fava beans, peas, green onions and 1 cup water. Bring to a simmer, cover and adjust heat to maintain a simmer. Cook until vegetables are tender, 5 to 10 minutes depending on size. If there is too much liquid in the skillet at the end of the cooking time, uncover the skillet, raise heat to moderately high and cook until some of the moisture has evaporated. You want the mixture to have a few tablespoons of tasty concentrated cooking juices at the bottom, but it should not be soupy. Season to taste with salt and pepper.

Cook pasta in a large pot of boiling salted water until al dente. Drain and transfer to a large warm bowl. Add remaining 1 tablespoon butter and toss to coat. Add contents of skillet and toss. Then add ¾ cup of the cheese and toss again. Serve immediately on warm dishes, topping each serving with some of the remaining ¼ cup Parmesan. Serves 4.

CONCHIGLIE WITH "MINESTRONE SAUCE"

THICK WITH WELL-COOKED VEGETABLES AND WHITE BEANS, THIS SAUCE CALLS TO MIND THE RUSTIC MIXED-VEGETABLE SOUPS WE ASSOCIATE WITH THE ITALIAN KITCHEN.

A LITTLE CHUNK OF PARMESAN RIND—THE PART THAT'S TOO HARD TO GRATE—ADDS RICHNESS TO VEGETABLE SOUP. NEVER THROW THE RINDS AWAY. JUST WRAP THEM TIGHTLY AND REFRIGERATE UNTIL YOU ARE MAKING VEGETABLE SOUP, BEANS OR A SAUCE SUCH AS THIS ONE.

- *3 tablespoons olive oil*
- *1 cup chopped yellow onion*
- *3 cloves garlic, minced*
- *1 large carrot, peeled and sliced (halve or quarter the thick end before slicing)*
- *1 large or 2 small celery ribs, sliced ⅓-inch wide*
- *3 ounces green beans, preferably Kentucky Wonder type, ends trimmed and cut into ½-inch lengths*
- *1 medium zucchini (about 3 ounces), ends trimmed, quartered lengthwise, and sliced ⅓ inch thick*
- *3 ounces cabbage, coarsely chopped or sliced*
- *1½ cups finely chopped canned plum tomatoes, with juice*
- *1½ cups chicken stock*
- *2 fresh thyme sprigs*
- *2-ounce piece Parmesan rind, optional*
- *Salt and freshly ground black pepper*
- *1 cup drained cooked cannellini beans (rinsed and drained, if canned)*
- *1 pound dried conchiglie rigate ("ridged shells")*
- *½ cup freshly grated Parmesan cheese, plus additional Parmesan cheese for passing*

🍃 Heat olive oil in a 12-inch skillet over moderately low heat. Add onion and sauté until softened, about 3 minutes. Add garlic and sauté 1 minute to release its fragrance. Begin adding vegetables, one at a time—carrot, celery, green beans, zucchini, cabbage—sautéing about 3 minutes after each addition. Add tomatoes, chicken stock, thyme, Parmesan rind (if using) and salt and pepper to taste.

🍃 Bring to a simmer, cover and adjust heat to maintain a simmer. Cook until vegetables are soft but not mushy, about 45 minutes. Uncover and stir in cannellini beans. Simmer until sauce has reduced to desired consistency, about 15 minutes. Remove and discard thyme sprigs and Parmesan rind. Taste and adjust seasoning.

🍃 Cook pasta in a large pot of boiling salted water until al dente. Drain. Transfer to a large warm bowl. Add sauce and toss. Serve in warm bowls, topping each serving with Parmesan. Pass more cheese at the table. Serves 4.

GNOCCHI WITH WHITE BEANS, TOMATO AND SAGE

A PASTA SHAPE WITH A HOLLOW IS THE BEST CHOICE HERE SO THE BEANS CAN SLIP DOWN INSIDE. IT'S IMPORTANT TO COOK YOUR OWN BEANS SO THAT YOU HAVE A FLAVORFUL BEAN BROTH TO ENRICH THE TOMATO SAUCE. ONCE YOU HAVE COOKED THE BEANS—WHICH YOU CAN DO A DAY AHEAD—MAKING THE SAUCE TAKES ONLY 20 MINUTES.

For the beans:

· *½ cup dried cannellini beans or Great Northern beans*

· *2 cloves garlic, smashed*

· *1 bay leaf*

· *½ yellow onion, sliced*

· *One 4-ounce piece slab bacon, ham hock or pancetta, optional*

· *¼ cup extra virgin olive oil, plus additional olive oil for garnish*

· *2 large cloves garlic, minced*

· *1½ tablespoons chopped fresh sage*

· *¼ cup minced parsley*

· *1 pound ripe plum tomatoes, peeled and seeded (page 22), then chopped*

· *Salt and freshly ground black pepper*

· *1 pound dried gnocchi or conchiglie rigate ("ridged shells")*

To prepare beans, soak them for 8 hours or overnight in water to cover by 1 inch. Drain. Transfer to a medium saucepan. Add smashed garlic, bay leaf, onion, pork (if using) and 4 cups water. Bring to a simmer slowly, skimming any foam that collects on the surface. Cover partially; adjust heat to maintain a bare simmer and cook until beans are tender, 45 minutes to 1½ hours, depending on age of beans. Remove from heat and cool in liquid. Drain, reserving liquid and discarding pork, bay leaf, onion and garlic.

Heat olive oil in a 12-inch skillet over moderately low heat. Add minced garlic, sage and parsley and sauté 1 minute to release garlic fragrance. Add tomatoes, drained beans and ⅓ cup of the reserved bean broth. Season highly with salt and pepper. Simmer gently until tomatoes begin to collapse and the tomato juices and bean broth coalesce into a sauce, 10 to 15 minutes.

Cook pasta in a large pot of boiling salted water until al dente. Drain. Transfer to a large warm bowl. Add contents of skillet and toss. Serve immediately in warm bowls, topping each serving with a generous drizzle of extra virgin olive oil. Serves 4.

Mixed Vegetable Sauces

LINGUINE WITH ROASTED PEPPER AND TOMATO SAUCE

WHEN YOU DRESS THE PASTA, THE NOODLES SOAK UP THE TOMATO SAUCE, LEAVING PRETTY LITTLE STRANDS OF ROASTED RED PEPPER WOVEN THROUGHOUT.

· *2 large red bell peppers, roasted, peeled, seeded and sliced into very thin strips (page 110)*

· *¼ cup olive oil*

· *4 cloves garlic, minced*

· *1½ pounds ripe plum tomatoes, peeled and seeded (page 22), then chopped*

· *4 anchovy fillets, minced to a paste*

· *¼ cup minced parsley*

· *Salt*

· *1 pound dried linguine*

· *1 cup freshly grated pecorino romano cheese*

Heat olive oil in a 12-inch skillet over moderately low heat. Add garlic and sauté 1 minute to release its fragrance. Add tomatoes, raise heat to moderately high and simmer, stirring often, until tomatoes collapse and form a thick, smooth sauce, about 10 minutes. Add a little water as necessary to keep sauce from sticking.

Stir in peppers, reduce heat to low and simmer an additional 5 minutes. Stir in anchovies, parsley and salt to taste. Keep warm.

Cook pasta in a large pot of boiling salted water until al dente. Transfer with tongs to a large warm bowl, allowing a little water to cling to the noodles. Add contents of skillet and toss. Serve immediately on warm dishes, topping each serving with a couple of tablespoons of grated cheese. Pass the remaining cheese at the table. Serves 4.

FARFALLE WITH LENTILS

✓ 9-20

A THICK AND HERBY LENTIL STEW WITH A SMOKY BACON FLAVOR MAKES A WONDERFUL PASTA
SAUCE. I LIKE THE WAY IT NESTLES IN THE FARFALLE "WINGS," BUT CONCHIGLIE ("SHELLS")
OR FUSILLI WOULD WORK WELL, TOO. THE LENTILS ARE DONE WHEN THEY ARE SOFT BUT STILL
HOLD THEIR SHAPE; YOU DON'T WANT LENTIL PURÉE.

- ¼ cup olive oil

- ⅔ cup minced celery

- ⅔ cup minced carrot

- ⅔ cup minced yellow onion

- 4 cloves garlic, minced

- 1 teaspoon minced
  fresh rosemary

- 2 teaspoons minced fresh sage

- 2 cups strained canned
  tomatoes (pages 21–22)

- 3 cups chicken stock

- 1 cup dried lentils

- 2 slices thick-sliced bacon,
  or one 3- to 4-ounce piece
  slab bacon

- Salt and freshly ground
  black pepper

- ¼ cup minced parsley

- 1 pound dried farfalle
  ("butterflies")

- ½ to ⅔ cup freshly grated
  Parmesan cheese

❡ Heat olive oil in a 12-inch skillet over moderately low heat. Add celery, carrot, onion, garlic, rosemary and sage. Sauté until vegetables are quite soft and sweet, about 15 minutes. Add tomatoes, chicken stock, lentils and bacon. Bring to a simmer, cover and adjust heat to maintain a simmer. Cook until lentils are tender and ingredients have coalesced into a flavorful sauce, about 1 hour. Uncover and stir once or twice to make sure lentils are not sticking to the bottom of the skillet. If sauce seems a little too thin, uncover it during the last few minutes of cooking to allow it to reduce. Remove bacon slices or slab bacon and discard. Season sauce to taste with salt and pepper. Stir in parsley. Keep warm.

❡ Cook pasta in a large pot of boiling salted water until al dente. Drain, reserving about ½ cup of the cooking water. Transfer pasta to a large warm bowl. Add contents of skillet and toss to coat. Add Parmesan and toss again, adding a little of the reserved water if necessary to thin the sauce. Serve immediately on warm dishes. Serves 4.

SPAGHETTI WITH ARUGULA, TOMATO AND AVOCADO

THIS RECIPE IS THE PERFECT CHOICE WHEN YOU WANT A LIGHT, WARM-WEATHER DISH TO ENJOY WITH A CRISP WHITE WINE. THE SAUCE IS ESSENTIALLY A SALAD OF ARUGULA, TOMATO AND AVOCADO THAT YOU TOSS WITH HOT PASTA. SAVE THIS RECIPE FOR WHEN YOU CAN FIND SMALL YOUNG ARUGULA WITH A MILD, NUTTY FLAVOR. THE PEPPERY TASTE OF OLDER ARUGULA WOULD BE TOO STRONG HERE.

THIS DISH WAS INSPIRED BY A SIMILAR RECIPE IN JULIA DELLA CROCE'S BEAUTIFUL PASTA BOOK, *PASTA CLASSICA*.

· *1 pound ripe tomatoes, peeled and seeded (page 22)*

· *½ pound arugula, coarsely chopped*

· *1 ripe avocado, halved, pitted, peeled and thinly sliced crosswise*

· *2 cloves garlic, finely minced*

· *5 tablespoons extra virgin olive oil*

· *2 teaspoons white wine vinegar*

· *⅛ teaspoon hot red pepper flakes, or more to taste*

· *Salt*

· *1 pound dried spaghetti*

Slice tomato halves very thinly. If tomatoes are large, cut the halves in half before slicing so slices aren't too long.

Place tomatoes in a large bowl. Add arugula, avocado, garlic, olive oil, vinegar, hot red pepper flakes and salt to taste. Toss gently, then let stand while you cook the pasta, stirring salad gently from time to time.

Cook pasta in a large pot of boiling salted water until al dente. Transfer pasta with tongs to the bowl containing the salad. Toss well, then serve on warm dishes. Serves 4.

BIBLIOGRAPHY

The following books and articles have inspired and enlightened me on the subject of pasta.

Bugialli, Giuliano. *Bugialli on Pasta*. New York: Simon & Schuster, 1988.

Del Conte, Anna. *The Italian Pantry*. New York: Harper & Row, 1990.

Della Croce, Julia. *Pasta Classica*. San Francisco: Chronicle Books, 1987.

————. *The Pasta Book*. San Francisco: Chronicle Books, 1991.

Giobbi, Edward. *Pleasures of the Good Earth*. New York: Alfred A. Knopf, 1991.

Hazan, Marcella. *The Classic Italian Cook Book*. New York: Alfred A. Knopf, 1976.

————. *More Classic Italian Cooking*. New York: Alfred A. Knopf, 1978.

————. *Marcella's Italian Kitchen*. New York: Alfred A. Knopf, 1986.

Kummer, Corby. "Pasta." *The Atlantic,* July 1986, 35–47.

La Place, Viana. *Verdura: Vegetables Italian Style*. New York: William Morrow, 1991.

La Place, Viana, and Kleiman, Evan. *Cucina Rustica*. New York: William Morrow, 1990.

————. *Pasta Fresca*. New York: William Morrow, 1988.

Plotkin, Fred. *The Authentic Pasta Book*. New York: Simon & Schuster, 1985.

Schneider, Elizabeth. "Extended Olive Branches." *Food Arts,* September 1993, 32–36.

————. "Olive Repertoire." *Food Arts,* October 1993, 34–39, 69.

Seed, Diane. *The Top One Hundred Pasta Sauces*. Berkeley: Ten Speed Press, 1987.

Simeti, Mary Taylor. *Pomp and Sustenance: Twenty-Five Centuries of Sicilian Food*. New York: Henry Holt, 1991.

Waters, Alice; Curtan, Patricia; and Labro, Martine. *Chez Panisse Pasta, Pizza and Calzone*. New York: Random House, 1984.

INDEX

TABLE OF EQUIVALENTS

The exact equivalents in the following tables have been rounded for convenience.

US/UK

oz = ounce
lb = pound
in = inch
ft = foot
tbl = tablespoon
fl oz = fluid ounce
qt = quart

METRIC

g = gram
kg = kilogram
mm = millimeter
cm = centimeter
ml = milliliter
l = liter

WEIGHTS

US/UK	Metric
1 oz	30 g
2 oz	60 g
3 oz	90 g
4 oz (¼ lb)	125 g
5 oz (⅓ lb)	155 g
6 oz	185 g
7 oz	220 g
8 oz (½ lb)	250 g
10 oz	315 g
12 oz (¾ lb)	375 g
14 oz	440 g
16 oz (1 lb)	500 g
1½ lb	750 g
2 lb	1 kg
3 lb	1.5 kg

OVEN TEMPERATURES

Fahrenheit	Celsius	Gas
250	120	½
275	140	1
300	150	2
325	160	3
350	180	4
375	190	5
400	200	6
425	220	7
450	230	8
475	240	9
500	260	10

LIQUIDS

US	Metric	UK
2 tbl	30 ml	1 fl oz
¼ cup	60 ml	2 fl oz
⅓ cup	80 ml	3 fl oz
½ cup	125 ml	4 fl oz
⅔ cup	160 ml	5 fl oz
¾ cup	180 ml	6 fl oz
1 cup	250 ml	8 fl oz
1½ cups	375 ml	12 fl oz
2 cups	500 ml	16 fl oz
4 cups/1 qt	1 l	32 fl oz

LENGTH MEASURES

⅛ in	3 mm
¼ in	6 mm
½ in	12 mm
1 in	2.5 cm
2 in	5 cm
3 in	7.5 cm
4 in	10 cm
5 in	13 cm
6 in	15 cm
7 in	18 cm
8 in	20 cm
9 in	23 cm
10 in	25 cm
11 in	28 cm
12 in/1 ft	30 cm